A Louisiana Sampler

Compiled
by

American Cancer Society,
Louisiana Division, Inc.

Baton Rouge
CLAITOR'S PUBLISHING DIVISION

Published and distributed by:
CLAITOR'S PUBLISHING DIVISION
3165 S. Acadian at I-10, P.O. Box 3333
Baton Rouge, Louisiana 70821

Dedicated

to

Ruth Boulet McCarthy

whose inner strength and courage

inspired

this volume of joy and warmth

– and a dash of humor.

We appreciate:

Mrs. Robert E. Birdsall .... *Cookbook Chairperson*
Garrett G. Stearns .... *Editor*
John L. McCarthy .... *Executive Vice President*
ACS Louisiana Division

The Area and Unit Cookbook Chairpersons who collected, tried, tested and took the time to assure the success of this venture so wholeheartedly.

Bob Birdsall .... *Cover Design and art work*

A special thanks to Bob and Ruth Birdsall whose tireless efforts have made this book possible.

FOREWORD

Last fall when the idea of a Division Cookbook first began to germinate a question arose as to the response—after all—there are already a lot of cookbooks. However cookbooks have been a very lucrative as well as a fun project in many Divisions of the American Cancer Society, so why not here in Louisiana where all these good cooks reside.

Never underestimate the enthusiasm of American Cancer Society volunteers! You are the greatest! In usual fashion the response has been overwhelming—the cooperation and the heartfelt good wishes for success from all areas of the Division have been tremendous.

In the selection of recipes the final decision had to be with the Tasting Committee, which has sifted, sorted, tasted and consulted with the experts. There were duplicates and near duplicates and we have double credited in some instances. Even so, we still have enough delicious recipes left over to publish another volume.

We are offering a departure from the regular cookbook set-up and believe we have something unique, a rare collection of the diverse tastes here in our State, but most especially a publication the Louisiana Division of the American Cancer Society can present with pride——A LOUISIANA SAMPLER.

Mrs. Robert E. Birdsall

Mrs. Robert E. Birdsall
Division Cookbook Chairperson

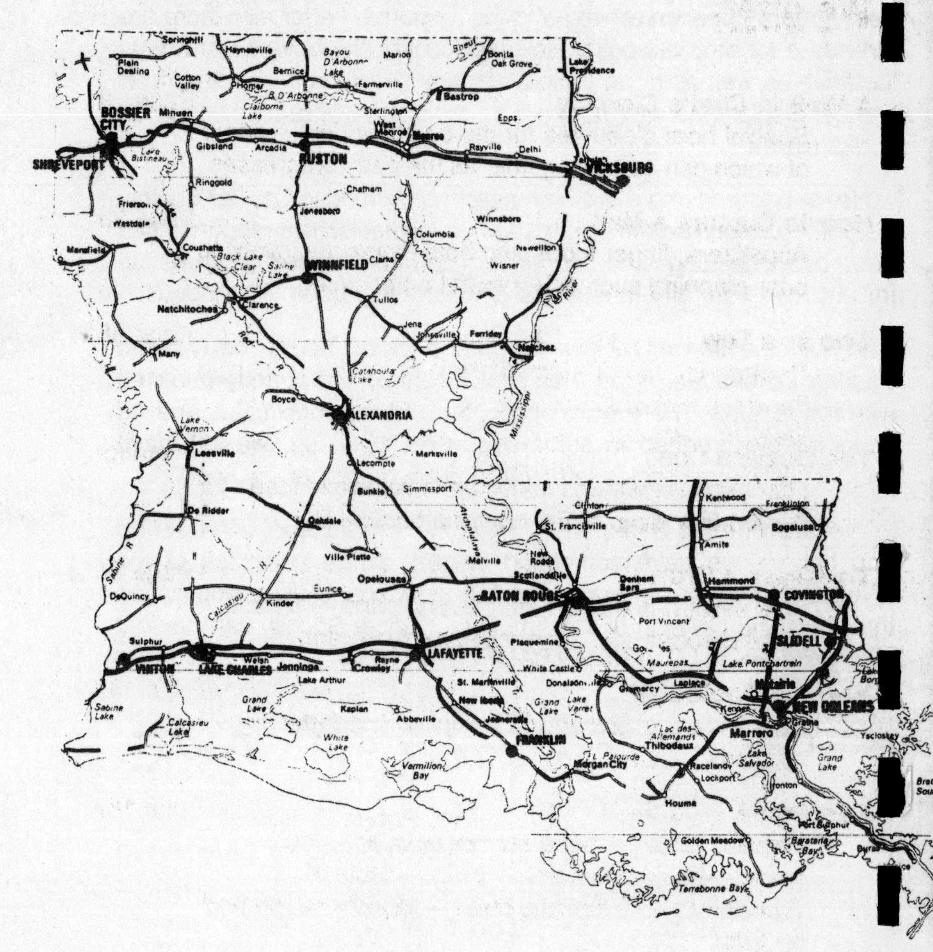

LOUISIANA DIVISION
AMERICAN CANCER SOCIETY

We offer:

A Wolf in Chef's Clothing

Notwithstanding today's feminine movement, this volume opens with the emphasis on the male population. It still holds true that many of the best chefs are men, so we do not intend to treat them lightly. Some of our favorite recipes have been here contributed most graciously by gentlemen cooks.

For the most part this section of the cookbook offers light or appetizer forms of hors d'ouvres, little bits of this and that without too much prior preparation which can be nibbled from one hand while balancing some form of libation with the other — mostly a way to set a meal in motion.

Included also are some splendid recipes which either make the party or are prepared as the party progresses and the good times roll.

Artichoke Dip

2 — 8½ oz. can artichoke hearts
2½ cups mayonnaise (Hellman's)
1 package Italian seasoning (Good Seasons)

Squeeze *all* moisture from artichoke hearts. Cut up artichoke hearts with scissors. Mix artichoke hearts and mayonnaise. Make day ahead.

Makes 20-30 servings.

David McCaleb
Shreveport

Avocado Dip

2 — 8 oz. packages Philadelphia cream cheese
1 large avocado (ripened)
1 green onion, chopped
1 teaspoon Worcestershire sauce
1 small can evaporated milk

Put all ingredients in medium sized mixing bowl. Mix at low speed until blended. Add more or less evaporated milk for thinner or thicker consistency.

Makes 1½-2 cups of dip.

Donna Messersmith Murphy
Harvey

Bacon Chrisps

Waverly Wafers
Parmesan cheese
Bacon strips, cut in half

Spoon cheese on cracker and wrap with bacon. Secure end of bacon on bottom of cracker (no toothpick needed).

Bake at 200° for 2 hours on broiler pan. Allow to drain.

Becky Gleason
Downsville

Coffee Steak

lbs. sirloin steak
stick butter or oleo
1 small bottle A-1 sauce
1 small bottle chili sauce
1 can mushrooms (optional)
1 cup black coffee
Paprika

Melt butter and sear steak on both sides. Place in large pan and sprinkle paprika on steak. Mix A-1 and chili sauce together, then pour over steak. If using mushrooms, add at this time. Bake 1 hour, 40 minutes in 350° oven. Remove and pour 1 cup of black coffee over meat mixture and bake an additional 20 minutes.

Serves 8-12 people.

NOTE: Leftovers are just as good the next day, if not better. The sauce is great over rice or potatoes.

Russell Wink
Jonesboro

Beef Sausage Stacks

— 3 oz. packages cream cheese
2 teaspoons prepared horse-radish
teaspoon chopped parsley
2 tablespoons grated onion
1 lb. smoked beef sausage, thinly sliced

Combine cream cheese, horseradish, parsley and onion. Mix well. For each "cylinder" spread 7 slices of beef sausage with cream cheese mixture, stacking them to form a cylinder. Top with a slice of sausage. Repeat for each cylinder. Wrap in waxed paper and chill 3 hours or more. When ready to serve, cut each cylinder into 6 or 8 wedges. Yields 7 cylinders or 42-56 wedges.

Marcelle Lorio
Hahnville

Cottage Cheese Dip

2 cups cottage cheese
¼ cup chopped dill pickle
½ cup grated cheddar cheese
¼ cup Italian salad dressing mix (dry)
6 tablespoons mayonnaise

Mix. Chill. Serve at room temperature with fresh raw vegetables such as celery curls, carrot sticks, cucumber slices or with Fritos or fancy crackers.

Makes 3-3½ cups of dip.

Tonia B. Cockerham
Trout

Crab Meat Appetizer

1 — 8 oz. package cream cheese
1 — 3 oz. package cream cheese
1 tablespoon Worcestershire sauce
1 or 2 tablespoons onion, grated
Pinch garlic salt
1 bottle tomato cocktail sauce
1 can crab meat, drained
Parsley flakes
Crackers, your choice

Blend first six ingredients in order listed and spread in bottom of glass pie pan. Cover with tomato cocktail sauce, spread drained crab meat over mixture and refrigerate overnight.

Before serving, top with parsley flakes. Serve as a dip with your favorite kind of cracker.

Makes 2-2½ cups of dip.

Audrey S. Maxwell
Jena

Crabmeat Dip

1 — 6½ oz. can crabmeat
1 — 8 oz. package cream cheese (soft)
1 tablespoon horseradish
2 tablespoons chopped onion
2 tablespoons milk

Mix ingredients as listed. Pour into container and bake 20 minutes at 350° just before serving.

Nelle Wilson
Jena

Crab Meat Toasties

2 tablespoons butter
2 tablespoons finely chopped green pepper
⅓ cup instant nonfat dry milk
⅔ cup water
2 egg yolks, beaten
½ teaspoon salt
1 cup (7½ oz. can) crabmeat drained and flaked
1 tablespoon finely chopped parsley
¼ teaspoon basil
6 thin slices of bread with crust removed

In a small saucepan melt butter; saute onion and green pepper until tender. Mix together nonfat dry milk, water, egg yolks and salt; add to saucepan. Cook 5 minutes, stirring constantly. Blend in crab meat, parsley and basil. Let cool. On baking sheet toast bread on one side; cut into squares, fingers, or triangles. Spread crab meat on *un*toasted side and bake 10 minutes.

Makes approximately 2 dozen toasties.

Mrs. Cliff Davis
Bossier City

Elephant Stew

1 elephant
Brown gravy
Salt and pepper to taste
2 rabbits (optional)

Cut elephant into bite-size pieces. This will take about two months. Cover with brown gravy and season to taste. Cook over a fire at 465° for five weeks.

This will serve 3,999 people. If more arrive, the two rabbits may be added, but do this with caution as most people do not like to find hare in their stew.

Alec Adams II
Ruston

Barbecued Franks

12-16 beef franks
4 teaspoons sugar
1 teaspoon celery salt
4 teaspoons Worcestershire sauce
1 medium onion, chopped
2 tablespoons butter
½ teaspoon hot sauce, or to taste
½ teaspoon white pepper
1 teaspoon prepared mustard
1 teaspoon paprika
½ cup catsup
4 tablespoons vinegar
¾ cup water

Saute the onions in the butter, then add all other ingredients except the franks. Bring to a boil and pour over the franks, which have been slit and placed in a baking dish with slit side up. Bake in moderate oven 350° about 20-25 minutes. Serve over hot buns.

Mildred Spears
Jonesboro

Bourbon Franks

1 — 14 oz. bottle catsup
cup bourbon
1 cup dark brown sugar

4 cups miniature cocktail franks
or 2 packages frankfurthers,
cut in 2" pieces

In large saucepan, mix all ingredients except frankfurters. Cover and simmer 2 hours. Add frankfurthers and heat. Pour into chafing dish and serve with cocktail toothpicks.

Makes about 64 servings.

Cynthia Kavanaugh
Ruston

Jezebel Sauce

1 — 8 oz. jar pineapple preserves
1 — 8 oz. jar apple jelly

1 — 8 oz. jar horseradish
1½ oz. dry mustard

Place in blender and blend well. Store in refrigerator. Serve with meats, etc.

Mrs. John S. Shatford, Alexandria
Alec Adams II, Ruston
Mrs. Jane Wroten, Winnfield

Mushroom Delights

2 lbs. fresh mushrooms
1 carton small curd cottage cheese
Hickory smoked salt

Wash mushrooms well and remove stems. Turn tops upside down; fill with cottage cheese. Sprinkle generously with the hickory smoked salt and place in broiler just long enough to heat thoroughly. Very delicious and filling. (Chop stems and save for seasoning spaghetti sauce.)

Makes about 20 servings.

Virginia Fontenot
Monroe

Marinated Mushrooms

2 teaspoons salt
1 teaspoon freshly ground pepper
4 tablespoons red wine vinegar
⅛ teaspoon garlic salt
Dash Tabasco sauce
2 teaspoons sweet basil
3 green onions, sliced
6 tablespoons olive oil
1 lb. can whole button mushrooms

Place salt, pepper, vinegar, garlic salt, Tabasco sauce and sweet basil in a large jar. Put on lid and shake until salt is dissolved. Add onions and olive oil. Drain mushrooms and add to mixture. Shake well and let stand at room temperature for 4 or 5 hours. Then place in refrigerator and allow to marinate for 2 to 3 days. Shake jar occasionally to keep flavors stirred up.

This makes a well-spiced marinade. For a milder one, dilute with some of the mushroom liquid. These are good served as hors d'oeuvres or in a tossed salad.

Mrs. James Patrick Giblin
Baton Rouge

Stuffed Mushrooms

Large mushroom caps
Pork sausage (Jimmy Dean mild)

Wash mushroom caps and stuff with sausage. Bake on a flat tray at 325-350° until meat is done (approximately 20 minutes).

Cheryl Jacks
Ruston

Bar-B-Que Onions

White flat medium onions
Oleo
Favorite barbeque sauce
Salt and pepper to taste

Peel onions, place each onion on a square of aluminum foil. Sprinkle with salt and pepper. Add 1 tablespoon barbeque sauce to each. Wrap each onion separately and either place on barbeque pit or in a 350° oven until soft.

Mrs. Frank (Jeannie) D'Autremont
LeCompte

Marinated Oysters

1 gallon oysters
6 ribs of celery, sliced
3 medium onions, cut in rings
1 large Wish Bone Italian style salad dressing
Dash of Worcestershire sauce
Tabasco sauce to taste
1 teaspoon lemon juice
Salt and pepper to taste

Drain oysters and combine everything in large bowl. Refrigerate while marinating for 1 full day.

Mrs. Raymond (Mary Lynn) Blanchard
Lockport

Barbecued Pecans

2 tablespoons butter or margarine
¼ cup Worcestershire sauce
1 tablespoon catsup
2 dashes hot sauce
4 cups pecan halves
Salt

Melt butter in large saucepan; add Worcestershire sauce, catsup and hot sauce. Stir in nuts; spoon into glass baking dish, spreading evenly. Toast at 400° about 20 minutes, stirring frequently. Turn out on absorbent towels and sprinkle with salt.

Makes about 25 servings.

Jewel Tison
Colfax

Salmon Loaf Dip

1 lb. can salmon
8 oz. package cream cheese
1 tablespoon lemon juice
2 tablespoons grated onion
1 teaspoon horseradish
¼ teaspoon salt
¼ teaspoon liquid smoke

Mix; form into roll and sprinkle chopped pecans and 3 tablespoons minced parsley on top.

Mrs. H. C. (Jeanette) Johnson
Pineville

Raw Vegetable Dip

½ cup mayonnaise
1 tablespoon Worcestershire sauce
1 tablespoon mustard
1 tablespoon lemon juice
1 tablespoon chili
1 teaspoon garlic powder

Mix all ingredients and chill at least 6 hours before serving. Dip with carrot strips, celery sticks, cucumbers, cauliflower and broccoli.

Makes 20-25 servings.

Anthony Zaunbrecher
Hayes

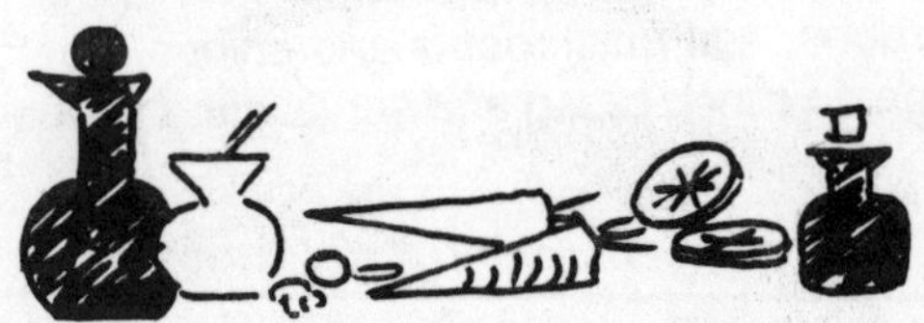

Fried Cauliflower

1 head cauliflower
1 or 2 eggs
Grated Parmesan cheese
Italian bread crumbs
Cooking oil

Boil 2½ quarts of water. Add cauliflower cut into flowerettes. Do not add salt. Cook for 10 minutes. Drain. Dip cauliflower into egg, then cheese and then into bread crumbs. Repeat for extra thick crust. Deep fry until golden brown.

Makes 6-8 servings.

Linda Giroir
New Orleans

Venison Bourguignonne

5 medium onions, sliced
½ lb. fresh mushrooms, sliced
3 tablespoons shortening
2 lbs. venison steak, cut in 1 inch squares
Flour to roll venison in
1 teaspoon salt
Garlic powder
¼ teaspoon crushed marjoram
¼ teaspoon crushed thyme
⅛ teaspoon pepper
1½ tablespoons flour
¾ cup beef bouillon
1½ cups red burgundy
Sliced French bread

Cook and stir onions and mushrooms in hot shortening till onion is tender. Shake garlic powder and salt on meat, roll in flour. Remove onions and mushrooms from skillet, put meat in and brown. Sprinkle seasonings over meat. Mix 1½ tablespoons flour into bouillon and pour over meat. Add wine and cover; simmer until meat is tender. If necessary to add more liquid; mix 2 parts bouillon to 1 part wine. When meat is done, add mushrooms and onions. Cook, uncovered 15 minutes. Toast French bread and serve with the above.

Makes 4 servings.

Dr. Charles E. Brewer
Jonesboro

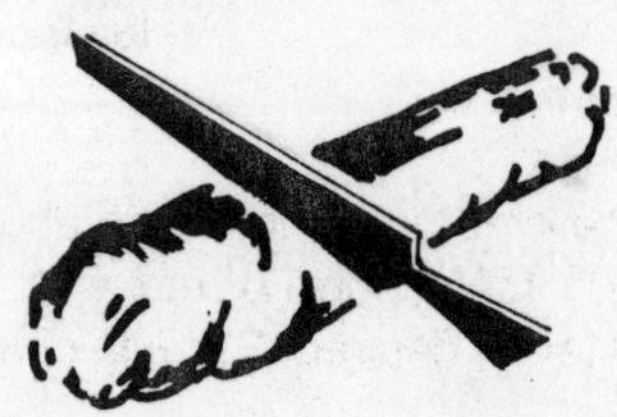

Kahlua

4 cups sugar
2 cups water
1 fifth bourbon or vodka
2 heaping tablespoons instant coffee
1 vanilla bean, split almost in half lengthwise
Piece of string

Boil water and add sugar and coffee; cool. Add the bourbon or vodka. Pour into ½ gallon bottle.

Tie string to the vanilla bean and suspend the bean in the liquid. Store for two weeks. At the end of two weeks, remove the bean.

Alec Adams II
Ruston

Hot Buttered Rum

1 pint vanilla ice cream
½ pound butter
½ teaspoon cinnamon
½ teaspoon allspice
½ teaspoon nutmeg

Blend butter with ice cream. Stir in all the above ingredients with an electric mixer. Use 1 tablespoon of mix with one jigger of rum in a cup. Add boiling water as desired. Stir with cinnamon stick. Add more rum if desired.

NOTE: This mixture makes a lot but keeps well in refrigerator.

Bob Birdsall
Jonesboro

A Few Hints on Serving Wine

Most articles written on the subject of serving wine have accomplished nothing more than to confuse and frighten the uninitiated and make him feel that if he must run the gauntlet of such agonizing ceremony and trouble to serve and enjoy wine, then he will take instead, a cocktail, a fizz or a sour.

It is true that certain prescribed rules for serving wines should be followed, but these rules are quite simple.

Serve wine in crystal clear glasses to appreciate the delicate colors, and never worry too much about the shape of the glass.

The glass should only be filled two-thirds full, thus making it possible to twirl the contents slightly and inhale the characteristic aroma of wine.

White wines are served cooler than sweet wines, cooler than natural. It is well to wrap a napkin around the wine bottle when serving to prevent the warmth of the hand from raising the temperature of the bottle and contents.

Never shake wine. If sediment is present, decant the wine carefully into another container so as not to disturb the sediment.

Never drink wine to quench your thirst. Wine should be sipped slowly to enjoy the taste and aroma.

The standing rule, white wine with chicken, fish, vegetables and young lamb while red meats, pork and game call for light red wines, can be changed without committing a social crime. If you only have one wine in the house, serve it by all means as tastes do vary.

The subject of serving wines, though interesting in itself, is secondary to the social dictum: Serve Wine! Whether or not the glasses be correct, the temperature proper or the occasion suited to the selection — Serve Wine!

How To Capture A Man

The old adage "the way to a man's heart is through his stomach" may not be as true as once upon a time, but men do still linger around the buffet table as can be noted.

Less frivolous hors d'ouvres – more downright plate and fork type foods are offered in this section, suitable for buffet parties and the like.

Here we have party food prepared with extra time and care before the gathering which leaves a relaxed hostess who can enjoy the fruits of her labor. Only she knows how tenderly she guards the table to keep the food fresh and the dishes replenished.

Party Artichoke Balls

2 cloves garlic, pureed
4 tablespoons olive oil
2 — 8 oz. cans artichoke hearts
½ — 9 oz. Italian bread crumbs
1 cup grated parmesan cheese

Puree artichoke hearts and garlic in blender. Add mixture to bread crumbs and cheese. Stir in olive oil. Add more oil if needed. Roll into individual balls using about 1 teaspoon mixture for each. Brown in oven 350° for 10-15 minutes.

Makes 4 dozen.

Donna Messersmith Murphy
Harvey

Artichoke Dip

1 cup Hellmans mayonnaise
1 can artichokes, drained
1 cup grated parmesan cheese

Put artichokes in food processor and chop until consistency of crab meat. Stir in other ingredients and bake in 350° oven until bubbly (about 20 minutes). Serve in chafing dish with thin rye crackers.

Serves 15-20.

NOTE: Most people tasting this think it is crab meat. I think it's difficult to dip with crackers and a knife in chafing dish is helpful.

Mrs. Leroy Vogel
Shreveport

Chipped Beef Dip

2 tablespoons butter
½ cup chopped pecans
Salt to taste
8 oz. package cream cheese
2 tablespoons milk
1 cup sour cream
2 tablespoons minced onion
2 tablespoons minced green pepper
½ teaspoon garlic salt
½ teaspoon pepper
1 jar (2½ oz.) dried beef, minced

Melt butter in a small skillet and saute pecans. Add salt, remove from heat, and reserve. Blend cream cheese and milk in a bowl. Add remaining ingredients and mix well. Turn into a lightly buttered casserole. Cover with the pecans and bake in a 350° oven for 20 minutes. Serve hot with chips or crackers.

Serves 8-10.

Mrs. M. Ann Cavanaugh
Leesville

French Beef Slice

1 loaf French bread
1 lb. ground chuck
1 — 11 oz. can cheddar soup
1 medium onion, chopped
1 — 10¾ oz. can tomato soup

Cut bread in half lengthwise; carefully scoup out inside, and break into bite-size pieces. Combine ground chuck and onion in a large saucepan or Dutch oven; cook until meat is browned. Stir in soup and bread pieces.

Spoon meat mixture into bottom half of bread shell and cover with top half of bread shell. Wrap loaf in foil; bake at 350° for 30 minutes. To serve, cut into slices.

Makes 8-10 servings.

NOTE: When French Beef Slice is served, all that's needed to complete the meal is a salad and beverage.

Mrs. Pat Painter
Lake Charles

French Pot Roast

5 lb. rump roast
1 garlic clove (mashed)
1 tablespoon chopped parsley
1 small can tomato juice
⅔ cup chopped carrots
½ cup chopped onion
½ cup chopped celery
½ cup dry wine
¼ cup brandy
¼ lb. sliced fresh mushrooms
½ teaspoon salt
¼ teaspoon black pepper

Brown the roast on all sides in a dutch oven or heavy pot. Pour off fat after thoroughly browned. Add the above. Cover tightly and cook over very low flame five hours or until tender. Remove roast carefully to foil and wrap to keep hot. Skim off fat from gravy. Add flour to thicken, about 2 tablespoons flour to 3 tablespoons water, salt and pepper to taste.

NOTES: Due to quality of meat, I have had this roast cook in less time, so do not over-cook.

Sometimes I use a de-boned roast, tied tightly. A regular rump with bone does very well as the bone does add flavor.

Edythe Fraser
Hodge

Hot Broccoli Dip

½ cup chopped onion
½ cup chopped celery
½ cup chopped mushrooms
3 tablespoons melted butter or margarine
1 — 16 oz. package garlic cheese, diced
1 — 10 oz. pkg. frozen chopped broccoli, cooked and well-drained
1 — 10 oz. can cream of mushroom soup

Saute onion, celery and mushrooms in butter until tender. Combine broccoli, soup and cheese; cook over low heat until cheese melts, stirring occasionally. Add sauteed vegetables to broccoli mixture, stirring well. Serve hot.

Sandra L. Theall
Abbeville

Caponata

½ cup olive oil
2 large eggplants, unpeeled and cut into ½ inch cubes
1 large onion, cut into thin strips
3 ribs celery, thinly sliced
1 can (1 lb.) whole tomatoes, drained
1 large clove garlic, minced
1 tablespoon sugar
1 teaspoon salt
1 cup green olives, chopped
3 tablespoons capers
2 tablespoons red wine vinegar
½ bell pepper, chopped

In a 12-inch skillet, heat ¼ cup oil; add eggplant, stirring a few times until cubes cook through, but still retain their shape; remove with a slotted spoon. To skillet add remaining oil and heat. Add onions, green peppers, celery; cook gently, stirring until wilted, about 10 minutes. Add tomatoes, garlic, sugar, salt, pepper, cook 10 minutes. Add the eggplants, olives, capers, and vinegar, cook 5 minutes. Cover and refrigerate overnight to allow flavors to blend. Serve as a first course on salad plate with crusty Italian bread. Makes 1½ quarts.

Mrs. Nada Natali
Iowa

Party Cheese Ball

4 cups shredded cheddar cheese
2 — 3 oz. packages cream cheese
⅓ cup mayonnaise
2 teaspoons sherry
1 teaspoon Lea & Perrin sauce
Pinch onion salt
Pinch garlic salt
Pinch celery salt
Chopped pecans

Combine softened cheeses, mayonnaise, sherry, Lea & Perrin sauce and salts. Blend with mixer or in food processor until smooth. Place in covered container and chill, until firm. Shape into ball. Roll in pecans. Cover and chill well. Serve with your favorite crackers.

Janice Beadle
Norco

Poultry In Wine Sauce

6-8 chicken breasts
½ cup cooking oil
1½ cup white wine
1 clove garlic, minced fine
1 onion, minced fine
2 teaspoons salt
2 teaspoons celery salt
¼ teaspoon cayenne pepper
½ teaspoon black pepper
¼ teaspoon dried tarragon
½ teaspoon dried thyme
1 tablespoon dried parsley
1 can button mushrooms, drained

Wash and salt chicken and arrange in rectangular dish. Combine all other ingredients except mushrooms. Pour over chicken and let stand several hours or overnight. Bake, covered for 45 minutes at 350°. Uncover, add mushrooms and bake 5 minutes more.

Makes 6-8 servings.

NOTE: Serve with wild rice and use sauce as gravy. This sauce may be used tor turkey also.

Jané S. Bolton
Jonesboro

Chicken Divan

2 — 10 oz. packages frozen broccoli
4 chicken breasts
2 cans cream of chicken soup
1 cup mayonnaise
1 tablespoon lemon juice
½ cup shredded cheddar cheese
½ cup cracker crumbs
2 tablespoons butter (or oleo)

Cook chicken breasts. Debone. Separate into 6 portions. Set aside. Cook broccoli according to package directions. Arrange broccoli in greased 11 × 7 × 2 inch baking dish. Place chicken on top. Combine soup, mayonnaise and lemon juice and pour over chicken. Sprinkle cheese on top. Combine cracker crumbs and butter. Sprinkle crumbs over top. Bake at 350° for 25 to 30 minutes. Garnish with pimento strips. Serve with a green salad.

Makes 4-6 servings.

Mrs. P.G. Cook
Ringgold

Crab Dip

½ stick butter
1 medium onion, minced
2 — 6 oz. cans crab meat with juice
12 oz. cream cheese
3 tablespoons chopped pimento
3 tablespoons chopped green onions
salt
Tabasco sauce to taste

Melt butter in heavy saucepan. Add onion and saute until cooked. Add crab meat and heat over low heat. Add remaining ingredients and heat until cheese melts and thickens. Refrigerate until ready to serve.

Serves 15-20.

NOTE: I always serve this dip with vegetable strips such as carrot sticks, celery sticks, cauliflower flowerettes, zucchini slices or strips and radish roses. My family likes these better than crackers or chips.

Cynthia Z. Nunez
Bell City

Crab Dip

1 stick butter or oleo
2 tablespoons flour
½ bunch green onions, finely chopped
¼ bunch parsley, finely chopped
2 cups evaporated milk
1 lb. crab meat
¼ lb. Swiss cheese
¼ teaspoon cayenne pepper
1 teaspoon salt
2 teaspoons Worcestershire sauce
Garlic powder
Onion powder

Melt butter in large sauce pan. Saute onions. Add parsley, flour, milk and cheese. Cook, stirring, until thick. Then add crab meat and seasonings. Serve hot in chafing dish with gourmet crackers or chips.

Janice Gautreau
Gonzales

Hot Crab Dip

½ stick oleo or butter
1 onion, finely chopped
2-3 ribs celery, finely chopped
1 tablespoon flour
2 — 8 oz. packages cream cheese
Salt and pepper to taste
Lemon juice to taste
Tabasco to taste
1 — 6 oz. can white crabmeat

Saute onion and celery in oleo until tender. Sprinkle flour over butter; stir in. Add cream cheese and salt, pepper, lemon juice and tabasco; mix well. Stir in crab meat. Heat through. Serve hot with cocktail crackers or corn chips.

Margie Morris
Leesville

Stuffed Crabs

12 hard-shelled crabs
2 tablespoons fat
1 teaspoon minced onion
2 tablespoons flour
1 egg yolk
1 cup milk
1 teaspoon horseradish
Dash cayenne pepper
1 teaspoon salt
2 tablespoons lemon juice
1 teaspoon Worcestershire sauce
½ cup bread crumbs
3 tablespoons chopped parsley
2 tablespoons minced parsley

Place crabs in boiling salted water for 20 minutes. Drain, break off claws, separate shells and remove spongy fingers and stomach found under the head. Pick out all meat and set aside. Clean upper shells thoroughly. Melt fat, add onion and brown. Blend in flour, add milk gradually, stirring until thickened. Add egg yolk, horseradish, chopped parsley, salt, cayenne and blend well. Add crab meat, lemon juice and Worcestershire sauce. Fill cleaned shells with the mixture and top with bread crumbs and minced parsley. Bake in 450° oven ten minutes or until well browned.

Mrs. Fred G. Anepohl, Jr.
Baton Rouge

Stuffed Crabs

1 stick margarine
1 onion, finely chopped
1 stalk celery, finely chopped
½ green pepper, chopped
1 lb. crab meat
2 tablespoons minced parsley
3 tablespoons chopped green onion tops
1 teaspoon Worcestershire sauce
½ teaspoon Tabasco
2 teaspoons lemon juice
1 egg, beaten
¼ cup milk
Salt and pepper to taste
½ cup bread crumbs (plain)

Melt margarine over low heat, add onions, celery and green pepper and let cook slowly until very well done. Add crab meat, parsley and green onion tops. Let simmer about 10 minutes. Add Worcestershire sauce, Tabasco, lemon juice and the egg which has been beaten with ¼ cup of milk. Season to taste with salt and pepper, and set aside to cool slightly. Add ½ cup of bread crumbs or more if desired and stuff the crab shells. Top with buttered crumbs. Bake at 400° for 15 to 20 minutes or until lightly brown.

Mrs. Olie Adams
Thibodaux

Stuffed Crab Shells

3 white onions, chopped
1 fresh tomato, chopped
¾ cup chopped green onions
3 ribs celery, chopped
3 cloves garlic
1 can Rotel hot chili tomatoes
1 can cream of mushroom soup
1 stick margarine or butter
Parsley flakes
3 lbs. crab meat
2 lbs. shrimp tails
3 cups French bread
3 eggs, beaten
Bread crumbs
Cayenne pepper
32 aluminum crab shells

Soak the French bread in the eggs. In a large saucepan saute the first seven ingredients in butter for ½ hour. Add remaining ingredients and mix well until heated through, about 15 minutes. Fill each crab shell with mixture; topping with bread crumbs and cayenne pepper. Bake at 350° for 30 minutes.

Makes 32 crab shells.

Westward Ho Club
Ponchatoula

Crab Meat Casserole

¼ cup butter
¼ cup flour
1 cup light cream
1 teaspoon salt
⅛ teaspoon black pepper
¼ cup sherry
1 lb. fresh crab meat
3 cups shredded cheddar cheese

Preheat oven at 425°. In saucepan melt butter, stir in flour, then cream, salt, pepper and sherry. Cook and stir over low heat until a thickened white sauce. Remove from heat and add crab meat. Pour mixture into a buttered 10 × 6 × 2″ baking dish. Sprinkle with shredded cheese and bake until cheese melts and mixture is heated through.

Makes 4-6 servings.

Mrs. Curtis Jemison
Mamou

Crab and Shrimp Dip

1 can claw crabmeat, drained
1 can small size shrimp, drained and diced
½ cup minced celery
1 tablespoon diced onion
½ cup mayonnaise
6 large eggs, hardboiled and diced
Paprika to taste
Garlic salt to taste
Season All salt to taste

Mix first 6 ingredients together and add last three to taste. Serve with buttery crackers or stuff into patty shells.

Makes 3 cups.

Mrs. Patty Meaux
Marrero

Crabmeat Spread

8 oz. cream cheese (softened)
6 oz. crabmeat (can or frozen), well drained
1 teaspoon prepared horse-radish
2 tablespoons milk
⅛ teaspoon pepper
⅓ cup toasted, slivered almonds
¼ teaspoon salt
2 tablespoons minced onion

Mix all ingredients together, except almonds. Spread in serving/baking dish or glass pie plate. Sprinkle with almonds. Bake in 375° oven for 20 minutes. Serve warm to spread on crackers.

Makes 1½ cups.

Gerry Lewis
Ruston

Eggs Brunch

16 eggs
4 slices bacon
½ lb. dried beef
1 can mushrooms
½ lb. butter
¼ teaspoon salt (optional)
1 cup flour
1 quart milk
1 cup evaporated milk
½ lb. grated cheese
¼ teaspoon pepper

Saute bacon till almost done, add dried beef, mushrooms. White sauce — melt ¼ lb. butter; while hot, add flour, milk and pepper; stir until smooth and thick. Mix eggs with salt and evaporated milk in ¼ lb. of butter. Mix meat in sauce and stir until combined. Butter casserole. Place small amount of sauce in bottom of dish; layer eggs on top of sauce; repeat sauce on top of eggs. Garnish top with cheese. Bake 1 hour at 275°.

Makes 12 servings.

NOTE: The dish can be prepared the day before if desired.

Donna Hines
Bunkie

Eggplant, Spanish Style

¼ cup olive oil
1 cup chopped ham
3 cups sliced onions
2 cloves garlic
2 pimientos, sliced
2 cups cubed eggplant
1 package frozen artichokes
1 — 28 oz. can tomatoes
2½ teaspoons salt
⅛ teaspoon pepper

Heat oil, cook onions, garlic, drained pimientos and eggplant until soft and transparent. Add ham, cook 5 minutes. Add tomatoes, artichokes, salt and pepper. Cook 15-30 minutes longer.

Makes 8 servings.

Doris D. Ledoux
DeRidder

Stuffed Grape Leaves

50-65 grape leaves, fresh or canned
1 lb. coarse ground lean beef
1 cup uncooked rice
¼ cup lemon juice
⅛ teaspoon cinnamon
Salt and pepper to taste
3 tablespoons butter or margarine

Rinse rice in cold water and drain. Add all ingredients with the exception of lemon juice and leaves. Mix well. Wilt fresh leaves a few at a time in hot water. (Hot water is kept near working area to do this.) Drain. Place a heaping teaspoon of mixture on dull side of leaf. Begin rolling as with a jelly roll. After first roll, fold in ends and continue rolling. This will be ½ to ¾" thick depending on size of leaf. Place a few leaves (unstuffed) in bottom of 2½ quart pan to prevent sticking. Arrange rolls in compact rows and barely cover with water. Sprinkle a tablespoon salt on top of the rolls and place a pottery plate over them so the rolls will remain in place. Cover pan and cook over medium heat for 15 minutes. Add lemon juice, lower heat and simmer an additional 15 minutes. Unmold by placing plate over pan and invert.

Makes 6-8 servings.

Mrs. Eddie Namie
Jonesboro

Best Guacamole

1 avocado (mashed with fork)
2 heaping tablespoons mayonnaise
2 dashes Tabasco or Louisiana hot sauce
Dash garlic powder to taste
Red pepper to taste
Salt to taste
½ fresh small tomato, diced
2 teaspoons Real Lemon (also may be fresh)

Mix and serve as a dip with doritos, tostados, fritos or as a salad on lettuce leaves.

Makes 2 or more servings.

NOTE: Will keep for several hours in refrigerator if sealed with plastic wrap.

Mrs. Fran Bass
Baton Rouge

Ham-Cheese Ball

2—8 oz. packages cream cheese
½ lb. mild cheddar or sharp cheese, grated
2 teaspoons grated onion
2 teaspoons Worcestershire sauce
1 teaspoon lemon juice
1 teaspoon mustard
½ teaspoon paprika
½ teaspoon salt
1 — 2¼ oz. can deviled ham
2 tablespoons chopped parsley
2 tablespoons chopped pimento
⅔ cup chopped pecans (chopped fine)

Soften cream cheese in large bowl. Add cheddar cheese, onion, Worcestershire sauce, lemon juice, mustard, paprika, salt, deviled ham, parsley and pimento; mix well. Chill until nearly firm. Shape into ball; roll in pecans. Wrap in foil; refrigerate overnight. Sprinkle with additional paprika if desired. Slice and serve.

Mrs. Olie Adams
Thibodaux

Kibbi

2 lbs. ground lean beef (chuck or round steak)
1½ cups finely cracked wheat
Salt and pepper to taste or 1½ tablespoons salt and ¼ teaspoon pepper
⅛ teaspoon cumin
½ cup ice water
1½ teaspoons chopped fresh mint leaves (optional)

Soak wheat 10-15 minutes in cold water. Drain off water and squeeze dry. Add this to meat and seasoning and mix well with ice water. Dip hands in ice water while kneading in order to soften kibbi. (Ingredients must be kept cold.) Run the mixture through a meat grinder one to three times for a finer consistency. To serve raw, serve with olive oil or Kibbi Topping.

Kibbi Topping:

¼ cup pine nuts or pecans, chopped
2 tablespoons butter or corn oil
2 medium onions, finely chopped
1 lb. coarse ground beef
Salt and pepper to taste

Brown nuts until golden brown. Then add meat and saute for 10 or 15 minutes. Add chopped onions, salt and pepper and cook until onions are limp. Remove from fire.

Mrs. Eddie Namie
Jonesboro

Kidney Beans Italianesque

2 tablespoons chopped onions
1 tablespoon butter
1 pound Provolone or Bel Paese cheese, grated
1 can pimentos, chopped
1 — 2 lb. can tomatoes
½ cup dry Sauterne wine
6 cups red beans, cooked and drained

Saute onions in butter and add grated cheese. When melted add beans, pimentos and tomatoes, then mix. Add wine and cook until cheese, wine and tomatoes are thick. Put in casserole dish and bake 1 hour at 300°

Makes 6-8 servings.

NOTE: Dark rye bread or pumpernickel is good to have with this dish.

Gladys Haynes
Wilson

Marinated Leg of Lamb

6 lb. leg of lamb, boned and butterflied
1 teaspoon coarsely cracked pepper
4 cloves garlic, sliced
2 tablespoons vinegar
½ cup dry red wine
½ cup olive oil
2 bay leaves
½ teaspoon dried tarragon
2 tablespoons salt

Spread lamb flat in a glass container. Sprinkle with pepper and garlic. Mix the remaining ingredients, add to the lamb and marinate in the refrigerator for 24 hours before cooking. Turn occasionally. Remove the lamb from the marinade and cook over very hot coals for 6 minutes each side. Meat should be well browned and crusty. Spread out coals to reduce the heat and continue cooking 6 to 7 minutes longer on each side for a total of 25 minutes. Slice as you would a steak.

Makes 8 servings.

Mrs. Bill Fuller
Kinder

Meat Loaf En Croute

2 cups grated day-old white bread crumbs
½ cup milk
¼ cup catsup
¼ cup chopped onion
1 raw egg
2 teaspoons salt
¾ teaspoon dried thyme leaves
¼ teaspoon pepper
2 lbs. ground chuck
4 hard-cooked eggs, shelled
2 dill pickles, quartered lengthwise
1 — 10 oz. package piecrust mix
1 raw egg yolk

Preheat oven to 350°. In large bowl, combine bread crumbs, milk, catsup, onion, raw eggs, salt, thyme and pepper. Mix well. Add ground chuck. Mix well. Place half of mixture in 9 × 5 × 3″ loaf pan. Line pan with aluminum foil. Place hard-cooked eggs lengthwise down center, gently pressing into meat. Arrange pickle slices. Then top with remainder of meat, gently packing into pan to cover eggs and pickle. Bake meat loaf 45 minutes. Cool at room temperature 15 minutes.

Meanwhile prepare piecrust mix as package label directs. Form into a ball on lightly floured surface, roll pastry to 18×12″ rectangle. Cut 4 inch strips from one end. Set aside. Turn oven to 435°. Drain meat loaf, invert in center of pastry. Bring all four sides of pastry over meat loaf; press edges to seal. Place loaf, sealed side down, on cookie sheet. Cut 8 strips from remaining piece of pastry, about ½ inch wide. Place strips diagonally across pastry. Gently press in place. With small cutter or knife cut three or four round holes, about ½ inch in diameter for steam vents. Brush pastry with egg yolk that has been beaten with 1 tablespoon water. Bake 30 minutes, or until top is golden-brown. Let cool. Refrigerate on serving platter.

NOTE: Sometimes I use 1½ lbs. chuck and ½ lb. sausage.

Mrs. Exie McDow
Quitman

Swedish Meat Balls

3 lbs. ground meat
Bread crumbs or stale bread
1 egg, beaten
Salt, pepper, garlic salt
¼ cup chopped parsley
¼ cup chopped green onions
1 small white onion, chopped
2 stalks celery, chopped
¼ cup chopped bell pepper
1 small jug Bar-B-Q sauce
1 can mushroom soup

Combine the first nine ingredients and roll into bite-size balls. Fry in small amount of fat. Pour off excess fat and add to Bar-B-Q sauce and soup. Pour sauce over meatballs. Serve in chafing dish.

Makes 100 servings.

Mrs. Glenn Alexander
Cameron

Mexican Dip

1 — 12 oz. can roast beef and gravy
1 can green chili salsa
1 package taco seasoning
Crumbled taco chips (until thick)
1 cup shredded cheddar cheese

Mix roast beef and gravy, chili salsa, taco seasoning in skillet. (This mix with roast beef is stringy.) Add taco chips until thick (but you don't want it too thick). Mix well. Pour into 8" or 9" pan and cover with cheese. Bake until cheese melts. Serve with taco chips.

Mrs. Marcia Williamson
Winnfield

Moussaka

3 medium size eggplants, peeled and cut into ⅜ inch slices
Salted water
Flour
½ cup cooking oil
¼ cup olive oil
¼ cup butter
2 large onions, chopped fine
2 lbs. ground beef
3 tablespoons tomato paste
½ cup dry red wine
½ cup chopped parsley
¼ teaspoon cinnamon
Salt and black pepper to taste
1 cup bread crumbs
1 cup grated parmesan cheese

Cream Sauce:

½ stick butter
4 tablespoons flour
2 cups milk
4 eggs, beaten
Nutmeg to taste
2 teaspoons lemon juice
1 carton cottage cheese

Soak eggplant slices in salted water 20 minutes. Drain, then blot on paper towels. Coat with flour. Preheat oven to 400°. Cover large baking sheets with foil and cover with cooking oil. Place eggplant slices on baking sheets, turning to coat well with oil. Bake about 15-20 minutes, then turn off oven and let eggplant stand in oven another 30 minutes.

Heat olive oil and butter in heavy skillet, saute onions until tender. Add ground beef and cook 10 minutes. Combine tomato paste, wine, parsley, cinnamon, salt and pepper and stir into meat; simmer and stir until all liquid has been absorbed. Remove from heat. Grease an 11×16 inch casserole (at least 2½ inches deep). Sprinkle bottom of casserole with bread crumbs.

Arrange alternate layers of eggplant and meat in casserole and sprinkle each layer with Parmesan cheese and bread crumbs to within 1 inch of top.

Cream Sauce: Melt butter in skillet, stir in flour and cook 1 minute. Add milk and cook until thickened, stirring often. Cool slightly, add beaten eggs, nutmeg, cottage cheese and lemon juice. Taste and adjust seasoning. Pour cream sauce over casserole and bake at 350° for 45 minutes or until golden. Cool slightly before cutting into squares.

Makes 8-10 servings.

NOTE: Freezes well.

Mrs. Bill Fuller
Kinder

Mushroom Rounds

Pastry:

2 cups sifted all-purpose flour
1 teaspoon salt
⅔ cup shortening
5-7 tablespoons cold water

Mushroom Topping:

1 lb. fresh mushrooms, chopped
¾ cup chopped onion
½ cup chopped celery
2 tablespoons butter
1 tablespoon lemon juice
½ teaspoon salt and pepper to taste
1 tablespoon cornstarch
¾ cup light cream
Shredded cheddar cheese

Make pastry and roll thin as for pies. Cut rounds with biscuit cutter and prick with fork. Bake 425° until light brown. Put rounded teaspoon mushroom filling on each and sprinkle with cheese. Heat in 350° oven until cheese melts. Pastry rounds may be made ahead stored in tightly covered container.

For mushroom filling, saute onion and celery in butter until clear, about 10 minutes. Stir in mushrooms and stir until liquid evaporates. Add lemon juice and seasoning. Shake cornstarch and light cream together and add. Cook over low heat until thickened.

Makes 50 rounds.

Mildred Spears
Jonesboro

New Year's Eve Party Squares

2 yellow onions, chopped
2 cups grated mild cheddar cheese
2 jars (small) marinated artichokes
4 eggs
6 crushed crackers
6 strips bacon, fried and crumbled
½ teaspoon cayenne
1 teaspoon garlic powder
1 teaspoon salt

Drain artichokes and save liquid. Saute onions in oil from artichokes. Mix all ingredients together and pour into a greased 8×8″ pan. Bake for 45 minutes at 350°. Cool. Refrigerate. Cut into squares.

Makes 30 squares.

Aline Roig
Chalmette

Green Noodle Casserole

1 large fryer
1 cup chopped white onions
1 cup chopped celery
1 cup chopped bell pepper
¼ lb. Velveeta cheese, grated
1 can mushroom soup, undiluted
1 — 4 oz. can mushroom pieces
1 small jar stuffed olives, sliced
1 — 8 oz. package green noodles

Boil fryer until tender and then debone and cut into bite size pieces. Cook green noodles according to package directions until tender. Cook in chicken broth and drain. Add rest of ingredients which have been thoroughly mixed and pour over chicken and noodles. Bake in 350° oven for 45 minutes or less until bubbly.

Makes 8 servings.

Ida J. Stovall
Jonesboro

Oyster Fondue

1 clove garlic
1 can oyster soup
½ cup milk
1¾ grated cups Swiss cheese
¼ teaspoon dry mustard
Pepper to taste

Rub fondue pot with garlic. Mix ingredients and melt in saucepan. Add mixture to fondue pot. Heat over low fire.

NOTE: Dip with French bread or toast.

Donna Messersmith Murphy
Harvey

Oysters Herman

24 select oysters (medium or large)
2 tablespoons melted butter
Flour for dredging oysters
¼ cup fresh lemon juice
1 cup A-1 steak sauce
2 tablespoons Worcestershire sauce
2 jiggers sherry or maderia wine

Salt and pepper oysters and dredge in flour. Brown on slightly buttered griddle or in a heavy skillet on top of stove. (Do not broil in oven.) To grill oysters until crisp and brown, additional butter or cooking oil may be used as needed. Place the rest of ingredients in a saucepan over *low* heat and heat thoroughly but do not allow to come to a boil. Blend 2 tablespoons flour into 3 tablespoons of water and stir in as thickening after sauce is heated. Correct sauce seasoning to taste by addition of A-1 sauce if too thin or sherry if too thick or highly seasoned. Place freshly grilled oysters on a hot serving plate or chafing dish and dress with heated sauce. Insert frilled toothpicks in oysters.

Makes 6-8 servings.

NOTE: Sauce can be saved, strained and used again.

Edythe Fraser
Hodge

Oyster Patties

1 — 12 oz. jar oysters, chopped
3 tablespoons butter
3 tablespoons flour
1 medium onion, chopped
3 green onions, chopped
2 tablespoons chopped parsley
3 cloves garlic, chopped
½ teaspoon allspice
3 dozen cocktail size patty shells

Simmer oysters in their own water for about 10 minutes. Saute onions and flour in butter until onions are soft about 5 minutes. Add water from oysters which have been drained. (More water might have to be added to arrive at right consistency; it should not be too thick.) Then add green onions, parsley, garlic and cook for about 5 minutes. Add chopped oysters, butter, allspice and salt and pepper to taste. Simmer for about 15 minutes and pour into patty shells. Place on cookie sheet and bake at 350° for about 10 minutes. Serve hot.

Alma H. Hemelt
Chalmette

Oyster Pie

3 tablespoons flour
3 tablespoons shortening
½ cup chopped onions
½ cup diced celery
½ cup diced green pepper
Oyster juice and water (2 or 3 cups)
1 cup diced potatoes
½ teaspoon thyme
1 teaspoon Worcestershire sauce
Salt, pepper, Tabasco
1 pint oysters
4 ozs. mushrooms
3 tablespoons sherry wine
1 can biscuits (8 oz. size)

Make a roux, browning flour in shortening to desired color. Add onions, celery and green pepper. Stir until wilted. Add oyster juice and water, potatoes, seasoning and cook 20 minutes. Add the oysters, mushrooms and sherry, pour into casserole. Top with biscuits cut in desired shapes. Bake at 400° until biscuits are done and golden brown for about 30 minutes.

Makes 6 servings.

Mary Cook
Husser

Black-Eye Pea Dip

¼ bell pepper, finely chopped
4 Jalapeno peppers, finely chopped
2 stalks celery, finely chopped
1 teaspoon black pepper
2 tablespoons Tabasco sauce
½ cup catsup
Salt to taste
3 chicken bouillon cubes
¼ teaspoon nutmeg
¼ teaspoon cinnamon
2 cans black-eye peas
½ can tomatoes
½ cup bacon drippings
3 tablespoons flour
Chips (potato or other kinds)

Mix together and bring to slow simmer — the pepper, Tabasco sauce, catsup, salt, bouillion cubes, nutmeg and cinnamon. Then add peas and tomatoes. Simmer 45 minutes. Mix together the bacon drippings and flour, add to peas and simmer another 10 minutes. Serve warm with chips.

NOTE: Best if made day before!

Jackie Burroughs
Shreveport

Party Peas

2 — 1 lb. 1 oz. cans LeSueur peas
1 onion, chopped
¼ lb. butter
1 can cream of chicken soup
1 cup grated sharp cheese
4 hard-boiled eggs, chopped
1 small can mushroom pieces
⅓ cup sliced almonds

Saute onion in butter. Mix all ingredients and pour in 3-quart pyrex dish. Bake in preheated oven 300° from 20-30 minutes.

Mrs. S.P. Border, Jr.
Shreveport

Superb Pate′

3 — 5 oz. boxes chicken livers, frozen
½ lb. braunschweiger
1 envelope green onion and dill dip mix
1 tablespoon sugar
1 tablespoon garlic salt
1 tablespoon milk
1 — 8 oz. package cream cheese

Broil livers 3 minutes, combine with braunschweiger in food processor (or chop finely). Blend till smooth. Combine with remaining ingredients. Cover with plastic wrap and chill several hours or overnight. Either roll or mound and serve with crackers or toast points.

Shirl Kamish
Haughton

Cajun Quiche

1 — 9-inch pie shell
½ cup mayonnaise
2 tablespoons flour
½ cup milk
2 eggs, slightly beaten
1 cup crabmeat
⅔ cup parboiled shrimp
1—8-ounce package Swiss cheese, diced.
⅓ cup chopped green onions

Bake pie shell at 350° for 15-20 minutes. Combine mayonnaise, flour, milk and eggs. Mix well. Stir in crabmeat and shrimp. Add cheese and green onions. Pour mixture into pie shell and bake 40 minutes or until toothpick inserted in center comes our clean. Serves 6-8, or more at a buffet.

Janice Beadle
Norco

Quick Cheddar Quiche

1 unbaked 9-inch pie shell
½ lb. bacon
4 ozs. grated cheddar cheese
4 eggs
1 tablespoon parmesan cheese
1½ cup milk, light cream or half & half
1 tablespoon flour
1 tablespoon butter
¼ teaspoon salt
Pinch nutmeg
Pinch cayenne pepper

Preheat oven to 375°. Bake pie shell about 10 minutes. Remove from oven. Fry bacon until almost crisp. Cut in 1″ pieces. Arrange bacon and cheese alternately in pie shell.

Put all other ingredients in blender and mix well. Pour over bacon and cheese. (To help keep oven clean, put pie shell on cookie sheet to catch spills.) Bake at 375° for 45-50 minutes or until knife inserted in center comes out clean. Cool in pan 10 minutes before cutting into wedges.

Makes 6-8 servings.

Caroline Webster Derbes
Luling

Beef Mushroom Quiche

1 unbaked pie shell
½ lb. ground beef
1 can mushroom soup
½ cup milk
2 eggs, slightly beaten
2 tablespoons chopped chives
¼ teaspoon salt
Pinch pepper
Dash red pepper sauce
¾ cup shredded Swiss cheese
4 ounces mushroom pieces

Preheat oven to 350°. Prick shell with fork. Cook ground beef. Mix soup, milk, eggs, spices and red pepper sauce with meat. Add mushrooms and cheese and pour into uncooked shell. Bake 45-60 minutes.

Makes 4-6 servings.

Linda R. Morgan
Jackson

Quiche Lorraine

2 — 9-inch pie shells
4 slices bacon, chopped
1 bunch green onions, minced
1 tablespoon butter
1 — 4 oz. can mushrooms, drained (or fresh)
4 thin slices ham, shredded
½ lb. Swiss cheese, grated
4 whole eggs
1½ cups Pet milk or ½ & ½
1 clove garlic, pressed
½ teaspoon salt
½ teaspoon dry mustard
Dash nutmeg
Dash black pepper

Prebake shells 10 minutes in 400° oven. Fry bacon until crisp; drain. Saute onions and fresh mushrooms in butter. Layer bacon, onions, mushrooms, ham and cheese in two shells. Combine eggs with remaining ingredients which have been beaten together well. Pour custard in filled shells and bake in 350° oven 35 minutes or until knife inserted in center comes out clean.

NOTE: Serves 6 as main course. Easily halved if desired.

Mrs. Warren S. Anderson
DeRidder

Shrimp Quiche

Crust:

8 ozs. cream cheese
1 cup flour
1 stick oleo

Filling:

¾ cup small cooked shrimp
1 egg
½ cup whipping cream
2 tablespoons finely minced green onion
½ teaspoon salt
¼ teaspoon dill weed
⅛ teaspoon cayenne
½ cup shredded Swiss cheese

Generously grease 24 muffin cups. Press dough into bottom and sides. Divide shrimp evenly among pastry shells.

Beat together egg, cream, onion, salt, dill and cayenne until well blended. Using about 2 tablespoons for each, divide among shells, sprinkle cheese over tops. Bake at 375° for 20 minutes or until golden brown. Cool 5 minutes and serve.

Mrs. Pat Painter
Lake Charles

Sausage-on-Rye Snacks

1 lb. hamburger
1 lb. medium hot sausage with sage
1 lb. Velveeta cheese
2 loaves party rye bread
1 tablespoon oregano
1 teaspoon garlic powder
1 teaspoon Worcestershire sauce

Cook hamburger and sausage until slightly brown. If too much fat, drain it off and blot out with paper towel. Add broken up Velveeta, oregano, garlic powder and Worcestershire sauce. Cook until mixed and no fat showing. Place party rye slices on cookie sheets and put generous teaspoon of mix on each little slice. Put cookie sheets in deep freezer until frozen and then into plastic bags or containers until needed. Bake in 350° oven about 15 minutes. Serve hot.

Adelaide Avotte
Hodge

Shrimp and Asparagus

2 large cans asparagus spears
½ cup Romano cheese
1 cup grated American cheese
2 tablespoons olive oil
3 lbs. cooked shrimp

Sauce:
1 cup white wine
2 eggs
1 tablespoon Worcestershire sauce
1 teaspoon Tabasco
1 teaspoon salt
1 can cream of mushroom soup

Grease bottom of casserole dish with olive oil. Layer with asparagus and cover with part of cheese. Layer with shrimp. Repear cheese, asparagus and shrimp.

Beat 2 eggs and mix Worcestershire sauce, wine, Tabasco and salt. Pour over casserole. Whip one can mushroom soup and spread over top. Sprinkle with bread crumbs and bake at 350° until cheese melts.

Makes 6-8 servings.

Ora Colvin
Jonesboro

Shrimp and Crab Curry

10 cups cooked rice
3 cups water chestnuts
2 lbs. cooked shrimp (or more)
1 lb. cooked crab
2 cups chopped celery
1 cup green onion (or plain)
1 cup pimento
½ cup parsley or dried parsley flakes
1 cup bell pepper

Sauce:
½ cup butter
¾ cups flour
1 quart plus ¾ cup milk
1 quart mayonnaise
1 teaspoon accent
¾ teaspoon curry powder
2 tablespoons horseradish
2 tablespoons lemon juice

First make sauce by blending flour with butter over low heat, add remaining ingredients, stir until well blended. Mix sauce with the first 9 ingredients, put into large pan about 4 inches deep. Bake at 350° until mixture is bubbly — about 30 minutes.

Makes 25-30 servings.

NOTE: Can be made ahead.

Mrs. Jack Shoemake
Oakdale

Marinated Shrimp

5 lbs. shrimp
Small onion, chopped fine
3 garlic cloves, chopped fine
3 tablespoons finely chopped parsley
½ cup finely chopped celery
Juice of 2 lemons
¾ cup Wesson oil
Dash salt
½ teaspoon sugar
Red pepper to taste
2 tablespoons creole mustard (or a mustard of any kind with horseradish)
1 teaspoon paprika for coloring
1 teaspoon steak sauce or catsup

Boil shrimp with salt, crab boil, onions and celery. Devein shrimp and set aside. Bruise next 4 ingredients well with a fork. (Best to bruise in a jar.) Add the last 8 ingredients. Add shrimp to sauce and chill before serving.

Makes 10 servings.

Ruth D. Wallace
Baton Rouge

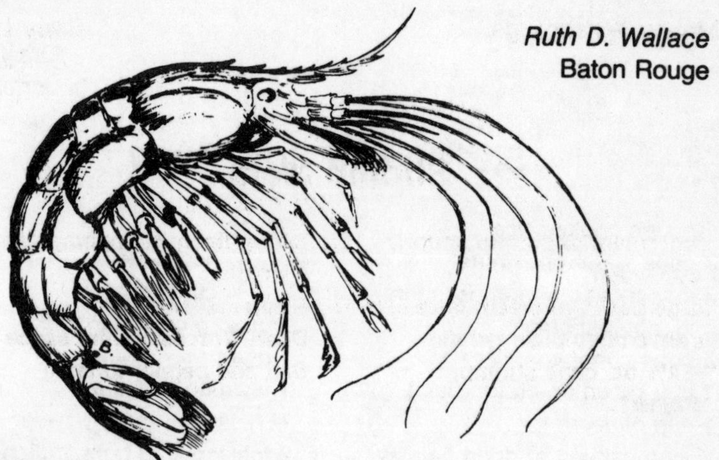

Note:

Did you say *five pounds* of shrimp??

Well, it may not be so easy to come by in this year of 1980, but we are going to hang in there with this yummy recipe until our abundant Louisiana yield returns to normal so that we can really gorge ourselves!!

The Tasting Committee

Shrimp Mold

1 — 10½ oz. can tomato soup
2 — 8 oz. packages cream cheese
1 cup mayonnaise
¾ cup finely chopped onion
¾ cup finely chopped celery
2 — 4½ oz. cans shrimp
½ cup hot water
2 packages unflavored gelatin

Bring undiluted soup to a boil. Add softened cheese and mix until smooth. Add mayonnaise, onion, celery and mashed shrimp. Stir until completely mixed. Dissolve gelatin in the boiling water. Add to other ingredients and mix well. Pour into a large jello mold and refrigerate. This takes at least four hours to congeal, and is best if made a day ahead. Invert onto serving dish.

NOTE: Good spread on crackers as an appetizer or on a bed of lettuce for a luncheon.

Gerry Lewis
Ruston

Shrimp Mold

1 can cream of shrimp soup
½ cup water
1 large package cream cheese
1½ envelopes plain gelatin
2 — 4½ oz. cans shrimp, drained
¾ cup finely chopped green onions
1 cup mayonnaise
Dash Worcestershire sauce and
Salt and pepper to taste

Bring soup and water to a boil. Add cream cheese and gelatin which has been dissolved in a little water. Whip together and cool. Add shrimp, celery, green onions and mayonnaise. Add seasoning to taste. Pour into mold and refrigerate. Serve with crackers.

Makes 50-60 servings.

Judith Zaunbrecher
Hayes

Shrimp and Noodles

1-1½ quarts shrimp (cleaned and peeled)
1 small package of noodles
1 cup chopped onion
2 cans cream of mushroom soup
1 cup chopped celery
1 cup chopped bell pepper
1 stick oleo
Parsley
Bread crumbs

Boil shrimp; clean and chill. Boil noodles according to directions. Mix vegetables, mushroom soup and shrimp. Add noodles. Sprinkle top with parsley and bread crumbs. Bake in slow oven for approximately 45 minutes.

Mrs. Bernard Rinker
Jeanerette

Spinach Balls

2 boxes frozen chopped spinach
2 cups Pepperidge Farm herb stuffing
2 onions, grated
¾ cup melted butter
¾ teaspoon garlic salt
½ cup parmesan cheese
½ teaspoon black pepper
1 teaspoon Accent
3 well-beaten eggs

Cook spinach according to package directions. Do not overcook. Drain well. Add the herb stuffing, butter, seasonings and eggs. Mix well. Leave mixture in the refrigerator until well chilled. Shape into small (walnut size) balls. Bake on greased cookie sheet at 350° for 20 minutes.

Makes 3 dozen.

Mrs. Tommie Poole, Jonesboro and
Mrs. Philip G. Cook, Ringgold

Wafers to Enjoy with Beer or Other Drinks

1 — 5 oz. jar Old English Sharp Kraft cheese
1 stick margarine (softened)
1¼ cups flour
½ cup chopped nuts
1 teaspoon salt
½ teaspoon cayenne pepper

Mix well (use hands). Roll into 6 separate rolls and refrigerate. When ready to use, cut into wafers about ½″ wide and bake at 350° for 12-15 minutes.

NOTE: Keeps in refrigerator for days.

Mrs. Ellis Roussel
Edgard

Mexican Wedding Cakes

1 cup butter or oleo
⅓ cup sugar
½ teaspoon almond flavoring
2½ cups sifted flour
½ teaspoon salt
1 cup finely chopped Brazil nuts
Red and green food coloring

Work butter and sugar in a bowl until creamy. Stir in flavoring. Stir in flour, salt and nuts and mix thoroughly. Divide dough in half. Stir a few drops of red coloring into one-half; green coloring into the other. Chill several hours. Form into 1″ balls. Place on greased baking sheets. Cover the bottom of a glass with damp cheesecloth and use it to flatten each ball into ¼″ thickness. Bake in a moderately low oven (325°) for 12-15 minutes or until the edges start to brown a little.

Makes about 3 dozen.

Sandra L. Theall
Abbeville

Never-Fail Mayonnaise

1 egg
2 cups oil
Juice of 1 lemon
Red pepper
Salt

Beat egg in mixer on medium speed. Add ½ oil in slow stream. Add lemon juice. Add rest of oil in slow stream. Add salt and pepper. Chill.

Variations: Add parsley or celery seed.

Mrs. David (Bel) Painter
Lake Charles

Mexican Mayonnaise

1 cup mayonnaise
1 cup oil
1 — 6 oz. can tomato paste
½ lb. or to taste jalapeno peppers

Blend ingredients together. Serve with crackers and chips.

Joyce Watt
Ruston

Buffet Hints

Let the food be the star — don't smother dishes in fussy garnishes.

Don't use substitutes.

Keeping the buffet food simple and the dishes freshly replenished offers a relaxed gathering for both guests and host.

Two Or A Few

When a family is small, the refrigerator is full—of leftovers! This is a pretty common place complaint, so we are offering in this section a few ideas sent in from around and about Louisiana — chosen to clear the serving dishes and give the cooks a chance to start over for the next meal.

It is a challenge to try for something unusual in these circumstances, perhaps one of the largest in the field of cooking. Here we have a few suggestions.

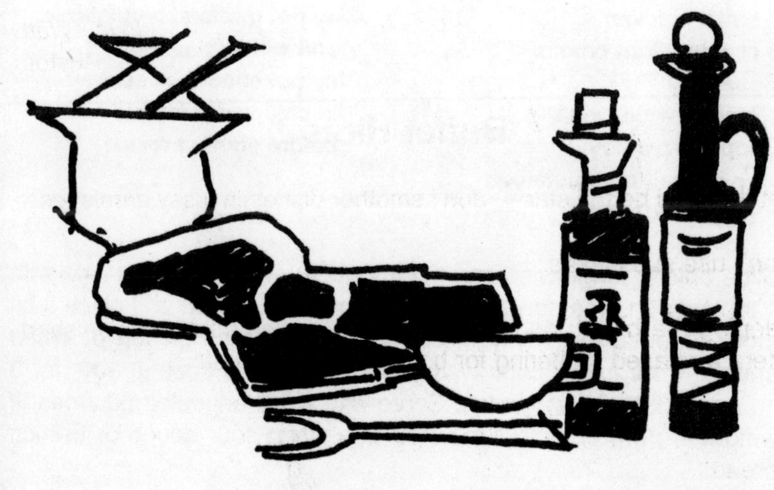

Cheese Souffle

1 slice white bread
½ teaspoon dry mustard
¼ teaspoon salt
¼ teaspoon cayenne pepper
3 tablespoons soft butter
1 cup hot milk
1 cup diced cheddar cheese
4 egg yolks
4 egg whites, beaten

Put bread, mustard, salt and cayenne in blender. Blend 5 seconds and then add butter, hot milk, cheese and egg yolks. Beat egg whites until stiff, fold in cheese mixture until lightly blended. Pour into 1½ quart, lightly buttered, souffle dish. Set in hot water. Bake 35 minutes in 375° oven.

Makes 4 servings.

Kathryn L. Dennis
Hodge

Etruscan Chicken

1 small chicken
3 or 4 medium onions
Rosemary
1½ cups white wine
Chopped parsley
7 or 8 small Irish potatoes (unpeeled)
Clay pot (preferably unglazed and with a clay top)
Clay pot should be soaked in cold water for two hours before starting recipe.

Slice onions lengthwise and put in bottom of clay pot. Sprinkle with 1 tablespoon rosemary. Salt and pepper the chicken and place a bit more rosemary in cavity of chicken. Set chicken on top of sliced onions. Pour in 1½ cups white wine. Cover and cook at 300° for 3 hours or 350° for 2½ hours. Serve with small unpeeled potatoes. If weight is no problem, also serve with warm sour dough or French bread.

Makes 2 servings.

Zach Hatcher
Clinton

Chicken Chinese

2 large skillets
2 boned breasts of chicken — (skinned)
Olive oil
¾ stick butter of oleo — (divided)
1 teaspoon powdered ginger
2 teaspoons cornstarch — (dissolved in chicken broth)
2 teaspoons brandy (or sherry)
2 teaspoons soy sauce
½-¾ red bell pepper
½-¾ green bell pepper
Arrowroot, some (dissolved in chicken broth)
Garlic salt
Sugar (pinch)
Chicken broth
Egg noodles
2 cups (or more) fresh mushrooms (sliced)

In one skillet: cut the breasts into 1″ cubes and saute with half of the butter and some olive oil. Add some chicken broth (if needed). Sprinkle ginger into skillet and add the cornstarch, sugar and brandy, mixing constantly. Set aside.

In other skillet: saute mushrooms and peppers (cut in strips) in butter and olive oil, add a little chicken broth, sprinkle in garlic salt and arrowroot. Simmer for a while, then add the chicken and juice from the other skillet. Heat altogether for a while turning chicken often. Serve over noodles with soy sauce at the table.

Makes 4 servings.

Robert C. Ewig
Shreveport

Country Style Chicken Kiev

⅔ cup butter
½ cup seasoned bread crumbs
2 tablespoons grated parmesan cheese
1 teaspoon each basil and oregano
½ teaspoon garlic powder
¼ teaspoon salt
2 chicken breasts, split
¼ cup white wine
¼ cup chopped green onions
¼ cup chopped parsley

Preheat oven at 375°. Melt butter in saucepan. On wax paper combine bread crumbs, parmesan cheese, basil, oregano, garlic powder and salt. Dip chicken in butter, then roll in crumbs. Bake 50-60 minutes. Add wine, green onions and parsley to butter. Pour butter and wine sauce over chicken last 10 minutes.

Makes 2 servings.

Liz Pecorino
Lake Charles

Chicken Laura

4 chicken breasts
1 large onion, chopped
2 cloves garlic, minced
1 rib celery, chopped
1 cup dry white wine
1 teaspoon salt
½ teaspoon pepper
1 tablespoon chopped parsley
Dash thyme
Dash tarragon
1 teaspoon basil
1 can beef broth bouillon
1 small can mushrooms
1 tablespoon flour
2 tablespoons olive oil

Brown chicken in olive oil, remove from pan. Add onion, garlic, and celery. Saute until tender. Add bouillon, wine, mushrooms and spices. Dissolve flour and add to pan. Cook on low heat until chicken is done.

Makes 4 servings.

Gregory Derbes
Luling

Ann's Baked Cornish Game Hens

- 4 Cornish hens
- ½ stick butter
- 2 onions, chopped
- 2 garlic pods, chopped
- 1 package onion soup mix (Lipton's)
- 1 small can bits/pieces mushrooms
- 2 tablespoons orange marmalade
- ⅓ cup white wine

Season hens with salt and pepper and McCormick Herb Seasoning, after patting dry on paper towel. Brown on breast first, then on back. Add onions and garlic until wilted, approximately 5-10 minutes. Cook on top of stove in Magnalite Dutch oven. Add 1 package Lipton Onion Soup Mix, mushrooms (drained) along with one cup of water. Simmer for 1 hour. During the last 20 minutes add 2 tablespoons orange marmalade and ⅓ cup white wine.

Anne H. LeJeune
Lafayette

Baked Slice of Ham

- 1 slice of ham, 1½ inches thick
- 12 whole cloves
- 2 tablespoons sugar
- 2 teaspoonfuls mustard
- ½ cup vinegar
- ½ cup water

Cut the fat from the ham. Stick the whole cloves into the meat. Place the ham in an enamel pan or glass dish. Cut the fat into bits and place it on top of the ham. Cover and bake at 400° for ½ hour. Then mix the sugar, mustard, vinegar and water. Pour this mixture over the ham. Cover and continue baking 1½ hours longer.

Makes 4-6 servings.

Mildred Spears
Jonesboro

Liver

1 lb. calf liver
2 tablespoons shortening
3 tablespoons oleo
2 tablespoons flour
2 tablespoons chopped onion
½ teaspoon salt
⅛ teaspoon pepper
1½ cups beef consomme
1 small can sliced mushrooms
½ teaspoon curry powder

Melt shortening in heavy skillet, brown liver, remove liver from skillet. Pour off all the fat. Add oleo to skillet with next seven ingredients. Make the gravy, slice liver in strips and add to gravy. Heat and serve over rice.

Makes 6 servings.

Mrs. Howard Hearne
Jonesboro

Po-Boy Sandwiches With Marchand de Vin Sauce

Individual French bread loaves or rolls
1 top round roast

Marchand de Vin Sauce:
6 small green onions, diced
4 tablespoons butter
¾ cup dry red wine
1 cup Franco-American brown gravy
Lemon juice (approximately ½ lemon)
2 large cans sliced mushrooms

Brown rolls slightly and split in half. Cook roast according to your favorite method, rare or medium, but season with salt and pepper and bar-b-que seasoning. When roast is done, allow to cool and slice paper thin.

Sauce: Saute green onions in butter until soft. Add red wine and cook rapidly to reduce the liquid to one half its original volume. Add brown gravy and lemon juice. Add mushrooms. Pile a generous amount of sliced roast on bottom half of each loaf; spoon sauce on top of meat and cover with top half of loaf. Serve immediately.

NOTE: This is great with slaw and sliced dill pickles.

Mrs. Robert Firnberg
Hodge

Green Pepper Steak

1 tablespoon soy sauce
1 clove garlie, chopped
½ cup oil
1 lb. round steak, cut in 1″ cubes
1 green pepper, cut in cubes
1 large onion, coarsely chopped
½ cup diced celery
1 teaspoon cornstarch
¼ cup water
2 tomatoes, coarsely chopped

Mix soy sauce, garlic and oil. Pour over steak. Let marinate 1 hour. Pour into frying pan and brown on all sides. Add green peppers, onion and celery. Cover. Cook 5-10 minutes over low heat. Then stir in cornstarch dissolved in ¼ cup water. Stir until thick. Add tomatoes. Cook another 5-10 minutes. Serve over rice.

Makes 4 servings.

Donna Messersmith Murphy
Harvey

Shepherd's Pie

1 pie crust (4 sticks)
2 tablespoons oleo
1 large onion, chopped
2 carrots, sliced
2 cups cabbage, chopped
1 lb. ground chuck
1 cup hot water
1 envelope instant brown gravy mix (¾ oz.)
2 tablespoons chopped parsley
1 teaspoon salt
½ teaspoon leaf savory
¼ teaspoon pepper
1 egg

Preheat oven to 400°. Prepare pie crust. Saute onions, carrots, and cabbage until tender. Saute meat, lower heat, stir in water and gravy mix. Add parsley, salt, savory and pepper. Cover; simmer 5 minutes. Add to vegetables. Roll pastry to a 16-inch round. Slide cookie sheet under pastry. Spoon meat and vegetables mix onto half of pastry. Fold other half over. Press edges together to seal. Crimp. (May be frozen at this point.) Mix egg with one tablespoon water, brush over top of pie. Make slits for steam. Bake (after thawing if frozen) at 400° for 30 minutes.

Makes 6 servings.

Sandra L. Theall
Abbeville

Easy Meat Loaf

½ lb. hamburger
½ cup grated raw potatoes
¼ cup grated raw carrots
1 egg, slightly beaten
1 teaspoon salt
¼ teaspoon pepper
½ teaspoon onion salt

Form into loaf and bake at 375° for 45 minutes.

Becky Gleason
Downsville

Pepper Burgers with Thyme Sauce

1 beaten egg
1 tablespoon milk
1 slice bread (crumbled)
½ teaspoon salt
¼ teaspoon ground nutmeg
½ lb. ground beef
½ cup chopped onion
2 teaspoons flour
1 cup beef broth
1½ teaspoons Worcestershire sauce
½ teaspoon dried thyme, crushed
1 medium green pepper, cut in strips
Hot cooked rice

In bowl combine egg, milk, bread crumbs, salt and nutmeg; add ground beef and mix well. Shape into 2 patties. In a skillet, cook patties over medium heat almost to desired doneness, about 3 to 4 minutes per side. Remove from skillet. Cook onion in skillet drippings till tender but not brown. Drain excess fat from skillet, blend flour and beef broth; stir into skillet along with Worcestershire and thyme. Cook and stir till thickened and bubbly. Return burgers to skillet; add green pepper strips; simmer covered till burgers are heated through, 2 to 3 minutes. Serve with rice.

Serves 2

Becky Gleason
Downsville

Stewed Rabbit

2 tablespoons baking soda
Cleaned rabbit, cut up
3 tablespoons oil
1 onion, chopped
2 cloves garlic
1 tablespoon chopped parsley
Salt and pepper to taste
Rind of half a lemon

Put baking soda in water to cover rabbit. Let soak ½ hour. Rinse well, dry with paper towels. Fry rabbit in oil until brown. Remove from pot. Saute, in same pot, onion, garlic, parsley, salt and pepper and lemon rind. Add rabbit with enough hot water to cover. Cook until tender.

Makes 4-6 servings.

NOTE: Serve with rice or creamed potatoes.

Nancy G. Giardina
Destrehan

"Ersatz" Shrimp Etouffee

1 can cream of onion soup
½ can milk
½ can water
2 teaspoons cornstarch
½ teaspoon seafood seasoning
1 can shrimp, drained and rinsed with cold water
Paprika

In saucepan mix cream of onion soup and water. Mix and shake cornstarch with milk and add. Cook over low heat until it begins to thicken slightly. Add seafood seasoning, dash of paprika and shrimp; heat to simmer. Remove from heat and serve over hot fluffy rice.

Makes 2 servings.

Mildred Spears
Jonesboro

Shrimp Fried Rice

¾ cup cooked and seasoned shrimp
2 eggs, beaten
4 tablespoons cooking oil
¼ cup green pepper and onion, chopped fine
2 tablespoons soy sauce
2½ cups cooked rice

Scramble eggs lightly in 1 tablespoon oil, set aside. In remaining oil, add green pepper and onion. Add rice and stir quickly so rice will not stick. Add 2 tablespoons soy sauce and cooked shrimp. Mix well, breaking eggs into small pieces.

Makes 4 servings.

Donna Messersmith Murphy
Harvey

Steamed Shrimp

½ lb. margarine
1 large onion, chopped
½ cup chopped celery
½ cup chopped bell pepper
1 tablespoon of Worcestershire sauce
Salt and pepper to taste
2 lbs. shrimp, unpeeled
1 bottle beer

Place margarine in saucepan and melt over low heat. Add chopped vegetables and seasonings and saute until tender. Add shrimp and cook about 5 minutes. Add beer; cover and steam about 15-20 minutes.

Jancie Beadle
Norco

Shrimp Stew

- 2 tablespoons oil
- 2 tablespoons flour
- 2 medium onions, chopped
- 2 cloves garlic, minced
- 1 tablespoon parsley flakes
- Pepper
- Cayenne
- 1 to 2 cups water
- 1 pound shrimp, peeled
- Garlic and onion salt to taste

Make dark roux, add onions, garlic, parsley and shrimp. Brown 10 minutes. Add water and seasonings and simmer for 45 minutes to 1 hour. Serve over rice.

Mrs. Elwanda P. Harvey
Leesville

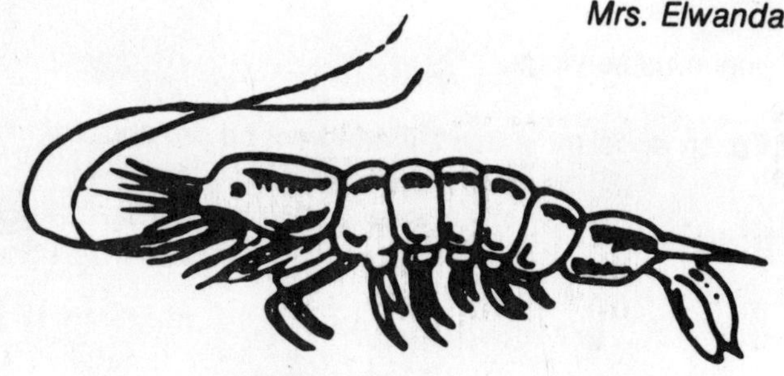

Crab-Ocado Cocktail

- 1 fresh avocado
- 1 cup cooked crab meat or
- 1—7½ oz. can crab meat
  drained and flaked)
- 1 cup diced fresh tomato
- ½ cup chopped celery
- 2 tablespoons lemon juice
- Salt to taste
- ⅔ cup seafood cocktail sauce

Cut avocado lengthwise into halves, remove seed and skin. Dice avocado, combine with crab meat, tomatoes, celery, lemon juice and salt. Spoon into individual serving dishes. Chill. Top with cocktail sauce just before serving. May be served on lettuce bed.

Makes 4 servings.

Nancy G. Giardina
Destrehan

Eggplant Casserole

1¼ cups peeled, cubed eggplant
9 saltine crackers, crumbled
¼ cup shredded sharp cheese
2 tablespoons chopped celery
2 tablespoons chopped onion
2 tablespoons chopped green pepper
½ tablespoon margarine, melted
¼ teaspoon salt
⅛ teaspoon pepper
¾ cup evaporated milk

Cook eggplant in boiling salted water for 5 minutes; drain. Combine with remaining ingredients. Turn into casserole. Bake in moderate oven (350°) for 40 minutes.

Makes 2 generous servings.

NOTE: If frozen eggplant is used, it need not be pre-cooked.

Mrs. Ralph W. (Charlotte) Baker
Greenwell Springs

Eggplant Slices

1 medium eggplant, unpeeled
3 tablespoons olive oil
1 tablespoon lemon juice
½ teaspoon oregano leaves
⅛ teaspoon cayenne pepper
Grated parmesan and/or romano cheese
Paprika

Cut unpeeled eggplant in half-inch slices. Arrange slices in single layer in shallow baking pan. Combine remaining ingredients except cheese and paprika. Spoon half of the mixture over the eggplant, and let stand for 15 minutes. Then turn the slices over, spoon on the remaining dressing, and let stand for 15 minutes. Sprinkle generously with the cheese and paprika. Bake in hot oven (400°) about 15 minutes, or until easily pierced with a fork.

Makes 2 servings.

Mrs. Ralph W. (Charlotte) Baker
Greenwell Springs

Pineapple Casserole

1—20 oz. can pineapple chunks
½ cup sugar
3 tablespoons all-purpose flour
1 cup shredded cheddar cheese
¼ cup melted butter or margarine
½ cup buttery cracker crumbs

Drain pineapple, reserving 3 tablespoons juice. Combine sugar and flour and stir in reserved pineapple juice. Add cheese and pineapple chunks, mixing well. Spoon mixture into a greased 1-quart casserole. Combine melted butter and cracker crumbs, stirring well. Sprinkle over pineapple mixture. Bake at 350° for 20 to 30 minutes, or until crumbs are lightly browned.

Makes 4-6 servings.

Hazel C. Gourgues
Hahnville

Squash Adoline

Squash, yellow crooked neck or zucchini
Salt
Pepper
Garlic powder
Basil
Oregano
Olive oil
Lemon wedges

Choose small tender squash. Scrub well, trim and half lengthwise. Place cut side up, one layer deep in baking dish. Dribble with olive oil. Sprinkle with seasonings to taste. Cover with foil. Bake at 350° until tender. Remove foil and allow to brown slightly. Serve with lemon wedges.

Adoline Perdue
Alexandria

Zucchini Fritters

1½ cups grated zucchini (approximately 2 medium squash)
2 eggs
⅓ cup Bisquick
½ cup grated parmesan cheese

Add the 2 slightly beaten eggs to the grated zucchini and mix well. Add the Bisquick and the grated parmesan cheese. Fry as pancakes on griddle. Serve with butter or sour cream.

Ruth Birdsall
Jonesboro

Zucchini Parmesan

4 or 5 small zucchini squash thinly sliced (about 3 cups)
2 tablespoons butter or margarine
½ teaspoon salt
Dash pepper
2 tablespoons grated parmesan cheese

Put zucchini, butter and seasonings in skillet. Cover and cook slowly 5 minutes. Uncover and cook, turning slices, till barely tender, about 5 minutes more. Sprinkle with cheese and toss.

Makes 4 servings.

The Tasting Committee

TOO BUSY TO COOK

In these busy days of hectic activity with so many cooks caught in the action, it was decided to offer a portion of the Cookbook to some of you.

There's no way to make the time go any slower, but sometimes we can make extra use with that which we have.

We came up with this little variety for you to mull over.

Barbecue Sauce

1 bottle (5 oz.) A-1 sauce
1¼ cups catsup
1 can (6 oz.) orange juice, undiluted

Mix ingredients in saucepan. Simmer 5 minutes. Ready for use or storage.

Donna Messersmith Murphy
Harvey

Blender Oatmeal Pancakes

1½ cups Old Fashioned Rolled Oats
¾ teaspoon baking soda
¾ teaspoon salt
1½ teaspoon baking powder
1½ cups buttermilk
1 large egg
1 tablespoon honey
3 tablespoons corn oil

In blender, combine all ingredients and blend about 30 seconds. Let stand 2 or 3 minutes, then bake on oiled griddle until golden. Turn and brown on other side. Serve with hot maple syrup or honey.

Makes 4 servings.

Mildred Spears
Jonesboro

Dotty's Jewett

6-8 pork chops
4 sliced potatoes
½ cup cooked rice
1 can string beans
1 can tomatoes
1 cup chopped celery
1 cup chopped onions
Salt and pepper to taste

Flour and brown pork chops. Put vegetables in casserole. Lay pork chops on top and cover. Cook 350° for 1½ hours.

NOTE: If you are in a hurry, cook for 10 minutes in pressure cooker.

Mary Joe Guillory
Monroe

Speedy Baked Chicken
(In Microwave)

2 tablespoons butter or margarine
3 lb. broiler-fryer, cut up
Pepper
Paprika
Salt

Preheat large browning skillet for maximum amount of time, according to manufacturer's instructions. Add butter. Arrange chicken with larger pieces at corners, skin side down. Place small pieces at center. Season with pepper and paprika, as desired. Cover with wax paper or plastic wrap. Cook in microwave oven, covered, on full power (high) for 12 to 15 minutes, or until chicken is tender. Turn chicken pieces over halfway through cooking time. Drain. Salt before serving, as desired.

NOTE: Gravy may be made from drippings if desired.

Makes 4 servings.

Doris McFarland
Downsville

Center Cut Chop Special
(In Microwave)

3 slices bacon, diced
1 cup finely chopped onion
2 cloves garlic, finely chopped
¼ cup soy sauce
3 tablespoons lemon juice
1 tablespoon honey
1 teaspoon chili powder
½ teaspoon salt
½ teaspoon curry powder
4 (¾ inch thick) loin pork chops (trim off fat)

Combine bacon, onion and garlic in 2 cup glass measure. Microwave on high for 4 to 5 minutes or until bacon is crisp. Combine with remaining ingredients except chops: set aside. Place chops in 2 quart (8×8) glass baking dish. Cover with plastic wrap. Microwave on *Roast* for 10 minutes. *Drain* and turn chops over. Pour seasoned sauce over chops. Recover and continue cooking on *Roast* for 12 to 15 minutes. Simmer for 15 minutes.

Makes 4 servings.

Becky Gleason
Downsville

Chinatown Chops

4 pork chops
1 package fried Rice-a-Roni
2 tablespoons butter
2 cups hot water
1—2 oz. can mushrooms
1 or more teaspoons soy sauce

In a large skillet brown 4 pork chops for 15 minutes and set aside. Brown 1 package of fried Rice-a-Roni with 2 tablespoons butter. Stir in 2 cups hot water, the mushrooms (undrained) and contents of vegetable sauce envelope in Rice-a-Roni package. Place browned chops on top. Sprinkle over each chop ¼ or more teaspoon soy sauce. Cover, brinç to a boil, reduce heat, and simmer for 15 minutes.

Mittie Jackson Pullig
Clinton

Spanish Rice

1⅓ cups pre-cooked rice
1 large onion, chopped
1 teaspoon chili powder
1 lb. (2½ cup) can tomatoes
1 teaspoon salt
1 large green pepper, chopped
1 tablespoon oil
⅛ teaspoon black pepper
1 lb. ground beef

Melt oil in pan with tight lid. Add ground beef and brown. Add vegetables and seasonings. Mix well. Add tomatoes; cover and cook slowly without stirring for 25 minutes.

Makes 6 servings.

Mrs. James G. Allison
Alexandria

Gone-All-Afternoon Stew

2 lbs. stewing beef, cubed
4 medium carrots, sliced
2 onions, chopped
4 potatoes, peeled and quartered
1 green pepper, chopped
1 rib celery, chopped
¼ cup sweet or sour pickle juice or cooking wine
10½ oz. can condensed tomato soup
½ soup can water
1 teaspoon salt
Sprinkle of pepper
1 bay leaf

Preheat oven to 275°. Put all ingredients in large casserole with lid to fit. There is no need to brown meat first. Mix ingredients. Cover; bake in preheated oven for 5 hours.

Makes 6 servings.

Dorothy Langley
Jonesboro

Quick Company Casserole

1 lb. ground beef
¼ cup minced onion
2 teaspoons salt
¾ teaspoon Tabasco sauce
1 cup raw rice
1 lb. can stewed tomatoes
1 cup hot water

Combine beef, onion, 1 teaspoon salt and ½ teaspoon Tabasco sauce; shape into 8 meatballs. Roll in rice; place in greased 2-quart casserole. Combine remaining salt and Tabasco sauce with stewed tomatoes; pour over meatballs. Pour water over casserole. Sprinkle with remaining rice. Cover; bake at 350° for 1 hour or until rice is cooked.

Makes 4 servings.

Linda Barrett
Wilson

Green Beans Almondine

2 packages (9 ozs. each) frozen French style green beans
¼ cup slivered, blanched almonds cooked in ¼ cup butter until toasted brown.

Prepare beans as directed on package. Toss gently with almonds and serve.

Makes 6 servings.

Carrie W. Hayes
Avoyelles

Sweet'n Sour Green Beans

2—1 lb.-4 oz. cans green beans
4 slices bacon, diced
1 small onion, sliced
¼ cup vinegar
¼ cup water
1 tablespoon sugar

Heat canned beans, drain, keep hot. Fry bacon and onions, stir in vinegar, water and sugar. Bring to boil. Pour over hot beans and garnish with onion slices.

Makes 6-8 servings.

Carrie W. Hayes
Avoyelles

Squash Casserole

12 yellow crookneck squash
2 medium onions
3-4 tablespoons margarine
1½ cups grated cheese
Salt to taste
Pepper to taste
Seasoned bread crumbs (Progresso)

Slice squash ½" thick and parboil in salt water until tender. In medium sized saucepan, saute sliced onions in margarine.

To prepare casserole dish: place one layer of sliced squash in a 2½ or 3 quart casserole dish, add ⅓ of the sauteed onions, add salt and pepper to taste, one tablespoon of the melted margarine (from sauteed onions) and ⅓ of the grated cheese. Follow the above procedure to make two additional layers. Top last layer with seasoned bread crumbs. Bake at 300° for 20 to 25 minutes.

Makes 9 servings.

NOTE: The squash can be prepared in a microwave oven following the directions for cooking fresh vegetables.

Cathy Kleinschmidt
Lake Charles

Vegetable Casserole

1 can mushrooms (small)
1 large package frozen mixed vegetables
1 lb. shrimp
½ teaspoon dry mustard
½ teaspoon Worcestershire sauce
Dash tabasco
1 can cream of mushroom soup
3 green onions, chopped
1 stalk celery, chopped
¼ green pepper, chopped
Sherry
Grated cheddar cheese and bread crumbs for topping

Combine all ingredients, except sherry and cheese. Pour into casserole. Save some whole shrimp for top. In addition, top with grated cheddar cheese and buttered bread crumbs. Cook at 400° for 45 minutes. Then add a little sherry over the top and serve.

Mary Joe Guillory
Monroe

Chocolate Sauce
(In Microwave)

2 ozs. unsweetened chocolate
1 cup sugar
⅛ teaspoon cream of tartar
1 small can evaporated milk
1 teaspoon vanilla extract
Pinch of salt

Place chocolate in a 2-cup measuring cup. Heat for 2 minutes (until it is melted). Stir until thick and creamy. Blend sugar and cream of tarter. Add milk gradually. Heat for 30 seconds. Stir. Heat for 10 seconds. Stir. Heat for 10 seconds. Stir. Blend salt and vanilla. Cool.

Makes 1½ cups.

NOTE: Excellent on ice cream. You may substitute ½ can of milk and 3 ozs. of dark rum. Also use with chopped pecans and whipped cream for hot fudge sundaes.

Mrs. Carl Ahrens
Oakdale

Pears Au Chocolate

For each serving: put 2 well drained pear halves together with ready-to-spread chocolate frosting. Stand upright in dessert dish. Chill. Just before serving, melt 2 tablespoons chocolate frosting and pour over pears. Top with dollop of whipped cream.

NOTE: Lovely and easy!

Shirl Kamish
Haughton

Baked Fruit

1 stick butter
½ cup brown sugar
1 tablespoon curry powder
Different canned fruits (peaches, pears, pineapple)
½ cup chopped pecans
Sour cream

Melt butter, stir in sugar and curry powder. Grease casserole, place in it the peach, pear halves and pineapple chunks. Bake until hot and bubbly. Serve with a big dab of sour cream and nuts.

Makes 6 servings.

Mrs. Reynolds Bath
Alexandria

Shirl's Quickie Dessert

1 box Jello gelatin, any flavor
1 pint cottage cheese
1 box Cool Whip (small)
1 can crushed pineapple, drained

Mix all ingredients together and store in refrigerator.

Shirl Kamish
Haughton

"Top of Stove" Bread Pudding

1 cup brown sugar
¼ cup raisins
4 slices bread, buttered and cubed
2 eggs (beaten)
½ cup granulated sugar
2 cups milk
Pinch salt
1 teaspoon vanilla

Spread the brown sugar in top of double boiler. Top with the raisins and add the bread, buttered and cubed. Mix eggs, milk, sugar, salt and vanilla. Pour this mixture over cubes of bread. Steam, covered, over medium heat for 1 hour. DO NOT STIR. Keep covered.

Shirl Kamish
Haughton

Dessert Salad

4 sliced bananas
1 can sliced peaches (16 ozs.)
½ cup chopped pecans
1 large box Cool Whip

Cut up drained peaches, combine with bananas, pecans and Cool Whip in a covered container and refrigerate. Can be served in 1 hour. This is a quick dessert and will keep for a day or two.

Makes 6-8 servings.

NOTE: Also to this recipe you may add cherries or coconut if you wish. However, I have found the combination of bananas, peaches and pecans very good.

Mrs. Printis Murphy
Oakdale

Pecan Pie
(In Microwave)

9″ pie shell, unbaked
4 eggs
1 cup brown sugar
1 cup light corn syrup
1½ teaspoons all-purpose flour
¼ teaspoon salt
1 teaspoon vanilla
¼ cup margarine, melted
1 cup pecan halves

Prepare pie shell. Set selector control to *Normal.* Cook for 4-5 minutes or until pastry is cooked. Cool. Prepare filling: in a 2-quart ovenware measuring cup or ovenware mixing bowl, beat eggs with wire whisk. Add brown sugar, corn syrup, flour, salt and vanilla. Beat with rotary beater until well combined. Beat in margarine. Continue cooking at *Normal.* Cook for 6 minutes or until mixture is thick, stirring every 1½ minutes. Turn into cooled pie shell. Place pecans on top, gently pressing into the filling. Change selector control to *Bake,* and cook for 2 minutes, turning after one minute. Cool pie completely on wire rack. Chill for 30 minutes before serving. Total cooking time—12 minutes.

Makes 8 servings.

Geraldine M. Knight
Leesville

Impossible Coconut Pie

2 cups milk
¾ cup sugar
½ cup biscuit mix
4 eggs
¼ cup butter
2 teaspoons vanilla
1 cup coconut

Use in blender only. Put all ingredients in electric blender and mix on high speed for 1 minute. Pour into greased 9″ pie plate. Bake at 350° for 45-50 minutes or until center is firm. The biscuit mix makes your crust and the coconut is the topping.

Linda Giroir
New Orleans

Southern Pralines
(In Microwave)

1½ cups firmly packed light brown sugar
⅔ cup half-and-half
⅛ teaspoon salt
2 tablespoons butter or oleo
1½ cups pecan halves

Combine sugar, half-and-half, and salt in a two-quart measuring cup (glass); mix well, stir in butter. Microwave at high for 7 to 9 minutes or until mixture reaches soft ball stage (235°)—stirring once. Stir in pecans and cool about 1 minute. Beat by hand until mixture is creamy and begins to thicken—about 3 minutes. Drop by tablespoonfuls onto waxed paper. Let stand until firm.

Makes 2 dozen.

Carol A. Jones
Coushatta

Peanut Brittle
(In Microwave)

1 cup peanuts
1 cup sugar
Pinch of salt
½ cup light Karo syrup
1 tablespoon margarine
1 teaspoon vanilla
1 teaspoon soda

Mix peanuts, sugar, salt and Karo in 4-cup glass measuring cup, stirring well. Cook four minutes on high. Stir, cook another four minutes. Add butter and vanilla, stirring well. Cook another ½ to 1 minutes. Add butter and vanilla, stirring well. Cook another ½ to 1 minute. Remove from microwave and add soda; stir well. Pour quickly onto greased cookie sheet. Let cool. Break into serving size pieces when cool.

Linda DeFreese Richmond
Ruston

Fried Shrimp Batter

1 cup flour
½ teaspoon sugar
½ teaspoon salt
1 cup ice water
2 tablespoons salad oil
1 teaspoon baking powder
1 egg

Mix all ingredients together and dip shrimp in batter. Coat well and fry in deep hot cooking oil.

Callie Jones
Coushatta

Shrimp Fried Rice

2 cups chopped cooked shrimp
¼ cup cooking oil
2 eggs, slightly beaten
1 — 4 oz. can mushrooms
1 teaspoon salt
Freshly ground black pepper
4 cups boiled rice
2 tablespoons soy sauce
½ cup onions, chopped

Fry shrimp in oil in deep frying pan for 1 minute, stirring constantly. Add eggs, mushrooms, salt and pepper; fry over medium heat for 5 minutes, stirring constantly. Add rice and soy sauce and fry for 5 minutes, stirring frequently. Mix with chopped onions.

Makes 6 servings.

NOTE: Diced cooked chicken, pork or ham may be used instead of shrimp (or all of these for a great taste sensation).

Mrs. Charles Hebert
Cameron

To Please A Crowd

The real test of our culinary skills can be activated when we cook for a large group — the entertaining today so often revolves around potluck parties, family gatherings and other bring-a-dish type of gathering.

This section really evolved from your contributions, and we have divided it into several parts to please you—

Breads

White Bread

5½-6½ cups all-purpose flour
2 packages yeast
½ cup warm water (105-115°)
1¾ cup warm milk (105-115°)
2 tablespoons sugar
1 tablespoon salt
3 tablespoons of margarine or shortening
Cooking oil

Spoon flour into dry measuring cup. Level off and pour measured flour onto wax paper. Sprinkle yeast into ½ cup warm water in a large bowl. Stir until dissolved. Add warm milk, sugar, salt and margarine. Stir in two cups of flour. Beat mixture with rotary beater until smooth (about 1 minute). Add one cup more flour. Beat vigorously with wooden spoon until smooth (150 strokes). Scrape side of bowl occasionally. Stir in 2½ to 3 cups of remaining flour gradually. Use enough flour to make a soft dough which leaves sides of bowl, adding more if necessary. Turn out onto floured board. Round up into a ball. Knead 5-10 minutes, or until dough is smooth, elastic and no longer sticky. Cover with plastic wrap, then a towel. Let rest for 20 minutes on board. Punch down. Divide dough into 2 equal portions. Shape into loaves. Place in 2 greased 8½×4½×8″ bread pans. Brush surface of dough with oil. Cover pans loosely with oiled, wax paper, then plastic wrap. Place pans of dough in refrigerator at moderately cold setting. Refrigerate 2-24 hours. When ready to bake, remove from refrigerator. Uncover. Let stand for 10 minutes at room temperature while preheating the oven. Puncture any surface bubbles with a greased toothpick or metal skewer just before baking. Bake at 400° for 30-40 minutes or until done. Bake on a lower oven rack position for best results. Remove from pans immediately. Brush top crust with margarine if desired. Cool on racks.

Yield: 2 loaves.

NOTE: The extra-easy cool rise method of bread baking opens the door to a whole new world of recipe possibilities.

Sister Mary Edmund Blackburn
Shreveport

Home Made Bread

2 cups lukewarm water
2 tablespoons sugar
2 tablespoons salt
4 teaspoons oil
Flour
1 package dry yeast

In large bowl add water, sugar, salt and oil. Add about 4 cups flour, sprinkle yeast and beat well. Add more flour until you can knead with hands. Knead well until there are no more bubbles. Use same bowl and let rise until it doubles its size. Cut in rolls in oiled pan and let rise till doubled in size. Preheat oven at 350°. Cook until brown.

Mrs. Eulla V. Guillory
Mamou

Nina's Basic Bread and Rolls

1 cup milk
¼ cup sugar
2½ teaspoonfuls salt
5 tablespoons shortening
¾ cup warm water
1 package active dry yeast
5 cups sifted flour

Pour milk into saucepan and heat to scalding poing. (Do not boil). Remove from heat. Blend in salt, sugar and shortening. Let mixture cool to lukewarm. Pour the ¾ cup warm water into a large mixing bowl. Sprinkle dry yeast into water and stir until yeast is dissolved. Add warm milk mixture to dissolved yeast. Stir in about half the flour and mix until smooth. Add the remaining flour and stir until dough is sticky and comes away from the sides of the bowl. Turn out the dough mixture onto a lightly floured board or countertop. Knead dough until smooth, usually 8 to 10 minutes. Dough will look smooth and satin-like. Place dough in a greased bowl, spread top of dough with soft shortening and cover bowl with a clean towel or waxed paper. Put bowl in warm place for dough to rise until double in bulk. Turn dough out onto a lightly floured board or counter top. It is now ready to be shaped into crescents, parker house, or cloverleaf rolls. Place shaped dough in greased pan. After shaping dough, cover and let it rise. Bake at 425° for 15 to 20 minutes.

NOTE: This recipe will make about 40 rolls.

Swedish Rye Bread

1 package yeast
½ cup warm water
2 cups rye flour
¾ cup Grandma's molasses
⅓ cup Wesson oil
2 teaspoons salt
2 cups boiling water
1 egg

Mix and set aside 1 package dry yeast and ½ cup warm water. Mix together 2 cups rye flour, ¾ cup Grandma's molasses and ⅓ cup Wesson oil and 2 cups boiling water. Add 2 teaspoons salt. Mix well and cool to lukewarm. Add yeast mixture, mix well and add enough white flour to make rather stiff dough (5¾ to 6 cups). Keep covered for 10 minutes. Knead 10 minutes on floured board. Place in greased bowl: cover and let redouble. Divide into 3 parts and let rest for 15 minutes. Shape and place on cookie sheet. Let rise 1 hour. Brush top with beaten egg. Bake at 350° for 35-40 minutes.

Mrs. John S. (Helen) Shatford
Alexandria

Whole Wheat Bread

2 envelopes active dry yeast
⅓ cup honey
1 cup water
2 cups milk
¼ cup margarine
1½ tablespoons salt
5 cups whole wheat flour
2-3 cups unbleached flour

Stir yeast and 1 teaspoon honey into warm water. Allow to proof 10 minutes. Heat in sauce pan the remaining honey, milk, margarine and salt. Pour into large bowl and cool to lukewarm. Add yeast mixture. Stir in whole wheat flour and enough white flour to make a soft dough. Turn out on a floured board and knead until smooth. Place dough in a buttered bowl, turn dough so buttered side is up. Cover with towel. Let rise 1 hour in a warm place. Punch down. Turn onto a floured board and knead a few times. Cover with bowl and let rise 10 minutes. Knead and shape into two loaves for 9×5×3 pans or four for small loaves. Let rise—covered. Bake about 40 minutes at 400°. Cool on racks. Bread is done when it sounds hollow when tapped.

Mrs. David (Bel) Painter
Lake Charles

Old-Fashioned Honey Wheat Bread

- 2 packages yeast
- 1 cup warm water
- 1 tablespoon salt
- ½ cup honey
- 2 tablespoons shortening
- 1 cup scalded milk
- 3 cups whole wheat flour
- 3 cups plain flour

Soften yeast in water. Combine honey, salt, shortening and milk. Cool to lukewarm, add yeast, add flour to make stiff dough. Knead on floured surface until smooth. Place in very large greased bowl and cover. (Will rise until double in size.) Shape into 2 loaves and let rise. Bake at 350° for 50-60 minutes.

Mrs. Ellis Fleming
Oakdale

Leo's Best Corn Bread

- 1 cup stone ground corn meal
- 2 tablespoons wheat flour
- 2 teaspoons baking powder
- ½ teaspoon salt
- ⅔ cup cold sweet milk
- 1 egg, beaten
- 1 tablespoon melted bacon drippings

Mix dry ingredients in bowl. Add milk, egg and bacon drippings. Grease a 6-inch skillet with 1 tablespoon of bacon drippings. Pour in corn bread mixture, heat on top of stove until bubbles form around the edge. Place in pre-heated oven at 400° and bake for 20 minutes. Turn out and brush top with melted butter.

Leo Abington
Coushatta

Grandmother's Cornbread

1 cup yellow cornmeal
1 heaping tablespoon shortening
1½ cups milk (half evaporated and half water)
2 eggs
1 teaspoon salt
1½ teaspoons baking powder
2 teaspoons sugar

Put cornmeal and shortening in bowl. Scald the milk and pour over the cornmeal and shortening. Mix thoroughly and add the remaining ingredients. Bake in a well-greased 8×8″ pan about 25 minutes at 450°.

Makes 6-8 servings.

Mildred Spears
Jonesboro

Honey Spice Bread

2 cups all-purpose flour or use half rye flour
1 teaspoon baking soda
1 teaspoon salt
1 cup milk
½ teaspoon cinnamon
1 teaspoon ginger
½ cup strained honey
1 egg, slightly beaten

Sift first three ingredients together. Add the balance of ingredients and beat mixture thoroughly 15 minutes at the very least if beating by hand. If using an electric mixer, beat 30 minutes. Long beating makes fine texture. Spoon into a buttered loaf pan, 9 inches by 5 inches, or into bread stick pans. Bake at 350° about 50 minutes for loaf or 25 minutes for sticks.

NOTE: Cut into thin slices, spread with unsalted butter and serve with tea or coffee.

Carrie Hayes
Avoyelles

Coconut Quick Bread

2 cups pancake mix
1 cup coconut
¼ cup sugar
¾ cup chopped pecans
1 teaspoon cinnamon
2 eggs
1½ cups milk
3 tablespoons butter, melted

Grease a loaf pan, line bottom with waxed paper and grease again. Combine pancake mix, coconut, sugar, pecans and cinnamon. Beat eggs; add milk and melted butter. Stir in dry ingredients and thoroughly mix until moistened. Pour batter in prepared pan. Bake at 350° for 50-55 minutes. Remove from pan and cool. Serve with whipped butter.

Whipped Butter:

½ cup butter
½ cup maple blended syrup

Beat butter until light and fluffy. Gradually beat in syrup.

Mrs. Charles A. Rogers
Cameron

Banana Bread

1 cup raisins, cooked and drained
2 cups sugar
1 cup butter or margarine
4 large eggs, well beaten
6 bananas, mashed
4 cups flour
1 teaspoon salt
2 teaspoons baking powder
2 teaspoons soda
1 cup chopped pecans

Cook raisins in small amount of water. Let boil until they puff up. Set aside and drain. Cream sugar and margarine well, add beaten eggs; add mashed bananas and blend well. Mix flour, salt, baking powder and soda. Add the dry ingredients slowly to cream mixture, beating all the time. Then add raisins and nuts. Pour into 2 well greased and floured loaf pans. Bake for about 1 hour and 15 minutes in 325° oven.

NOTE: Do not overbake, but be sure toothpick comes out clean when tested.

Icing:

2 tablespoons butter or margarine
½ cup brown sugar
½ cup milk
1½ cup powdered sugar

Using small pan, bring butter, brown sugar and milk to rolling boil, stirring all the time. Remove from heat and allow to cool slightly. Add powdered sugar. Beat with mixer until thick enough to spread. Add additional powdered sugar if necessary.

Mrs. Olie Adams
Thibodeaux

Monkey Bread

1 envelope active dry yeast
or 1 cake compressed yeast
½ cup very warm water
1 cup (2 sticks) butter or margarine
¼ cup sugar
1 teaspoon salt
½ cup evaporated milk
3½ cups sifted regular flour

Sprinkle or crumble yeast into very warm water in a large bowl. Stir until yeast dissolves. Melt ½ cup of the butter or margarine in small saucepan. Stir in sugar, salt and evaporated milk until sugar dissolves. Stir into yeast mixture.Beat in flour all at once until batter is smooth and very stiff, then knead until shiny-elastic. Cover with a clean towel, let rise in a warm place, away from draft, one hour or until double in bulk. Melt remaining ½ cup butter or margarine in a small saucepan. Punch dough down; roll out to a rectangle, 18x12" on a lightly floured pastry cloth or board, cut into diamond shapes with a 3" cutter. Dip each piece in melted butter or margarine to coat both sides; place, overlapping, in layers in an ungreased 12-cup tube mold. Bake in moderate oven (350°) 45 minutes or until golden brown. (A loaf gives a hollow sound when tapped.) Remove from mold. Serve warm.

Mrs. Virginia Cabble
Bunkie

Oatmeal Bread

1 cup oatmeal
2 packages yeast
1 tablespoon salt
½ cup honey
2 tablespoons cooking oil
6 cups plain flour

Soak oatmeal in 2 cups boiling water until lukewarm. Dissolve yeast in ⅓ cup warm water. Add yeast, salt, honey and cooking oil to oatmeal, Add flour, knead until smooth. Place in greased bowl, cover and let rise until double in size. Place in 2 loaf pans or bundt pan. Let rise about 2 hours. Bake at 325° for about 50 minutes.

Mrs. Ellis Fleming
Oakdale

Yam Bread

3½ cups flour
3 cups sugar
1 teaspoon salt
2 teaspoons soda
1 teaspoon cinnamon
1 teaspoon cloves
2 cups sweet potatoes, boiled and mashed (or canned)
1 cup cooking oil
⅔ cup water
4 eggs, well beaten
1 cup chopped pecans
1 cup chopped dates or raisins

Sift the dry ingredients together. Add the potatoes, cooking oil and water. Beat in the eggs, one at a time. Stir in nuts and dates. Grease and flour four 1-lb. coffee cans. Divide the batter equally among the four cans, and bake 1 hour at 350°. Allow to cool in the cans before turning out.

LaVerne Nalley
Quitman

Zucchini Bread

3 eggs, beaten
2 cups sugar
1 cup oil
2 cups grated zucchini
2 cups flour
1 teaspoon soda
1 teaspoon salt
2 tablespoons vanilla
1 cup chopped nuts

Combine ingredients and bake at 350° for 1 hour.

Virginia McCaa Bond
Keithville

Beer Biscuits

2 cups biscuit mix
¼ cup sugar
1 cup beer

Mix all ingredients. Pour into greased muffin tins. Let rise 30 minutes. Bake at 375° for 30 minutes.

Bee Troxler
Hahnville

Tante Yeah's "White Goose" Biscuits

2 cups White Goose flour
½ teaspoon salt
½ cup fresh milk
½ cup fresh lard with crackling crumbs
2½ teaspoons baking powder

Mix all ingredients in bowl. Roll out dough on lightly floured board and cut biscuits with biscuit cutter. Place in greased pan. Bake at 375° until brown.

Mrs. O.P. Bordelon
Moreauville

Company Rolls

1 cup shortening
1 cup sugar
1 cup boiling water
2 cakes yeast
2 well beaten eggs
6 cups flour
1 teaspoon salt

Cream one cup shortening with 1 cup sugar; add 1 cup boiling water and allow mixture to cool. Dissolve 2 cakes of yeast in 1 cup cold water and stir in, along with 2 well beaten eggs, and 6 or more cups flour that has been sifted with 1 teaspoon salt. Cover dough and place in refrigerator overnight. Take out next morning and make into rolls. Let rise about 3 hours and bake in slow oven (300°) until golden brown.

NOTE: Delicious! (Will keep refrigerated for 10 days.)

Clarice Madden
Ringgold

Mayonnaise Rolls

1 cup flour
½ teaspoon baking powder
¾ cup milk
½ teaspoon salt
1 tablespoon mayonnaise

Mix all ingredients and bake in muffin tins at 400° until brown.

Mrs. Charles A. Rogers
Cameron

Parsley Rolls

½ cup real butter (melted)
1½ teaspoons parsley flakes
½ teaspoon dill weed
1 tablespoon onion flakes
2 tablespoons parmesan cheese
1 can buttermilk biscuits

(Recipe makes enough butter for 2 cans biscuits; use ½ recipe for 1 can.)

Melt butter in 9″ square pan. Mix herbs together and mix with butter. Let stand 30 minutes; then swish in biscuits (cut in ½ or ¼) and bake at 425° for 12-15 minutes.

Linda Tyrone
Caddo

Sweet Rolls

1 piece wet yeast or 1 — ¼-oz. package dry active yeast
½ cup sugar
1 cup lukewarm water
4 cups all-purpose flour
½ teaspoon salt
1 cup butter
2 eggs

Dissolve yeast and 1 teaspoon sugar in lukewarm water and set aside. In large bowl, mix flour, salt and remaining sugar. Cut in butter, stir in eggs and dissolved yeast. Cover and let rise about 1½ hours before serving time. Shape into rolls and place in well greased muffin pans. Put in warm place and let rise to double in size. Preheat oven to 400°. Brush tops with melted butter and bake 10 to 12 minutes.

Makes 24 rolls.

Mrs. Marine H. Dupas
Moreauville

Sweet Potato Muffins

2 fresh eggs
1 stick butter
1¼ cups granulated sugar
1 cup milk
1½ cups all-purpose flour
2 teaspoons baking powder
1 teaspoon cinnamon
¼ teaspoon nutmeg
¼ teaspoon salt
1½ cups sweet potatoes, mashed
½ cup chopped raisins
¼ cup pecans or walnuts, chopped

Have all ingredients at room temperature. Cream butter, sugar and sweet potatoes until smooth. Add eggs. Blend all 4 ingredients well. Sift flour, baking powder, and spices and add alternately with milk to the egg batter. Do not overmix. Fold in nuts and raisins last. Sprinkle a little cinnamon-sugar on top before baking. Bake in greased muffin tins at 400° for approximately 25 minutes or until done. You should get about 2 dozen small muffins from above batch.

NOTE: Muffins can be frozen and reheated.

Mrs. Milton Goins
Leesville

Fresh Apple Coffee Cake

2 large apples
1½ cups flour (before sifting)
½ cup Wesson oil
1 cup sugar
1 egg
½ teaspoon allspice
½ teaspoon cinnamon
1 teaspoon soda
¼ teaspoon salt
½ cup chopped nuts

Sift flour. Dice apples, leaving peeling on, and cover with 1 cup sugar for 20 minutes. To apple mixture add egg and Wesson oil. Mix well. Sift dry ingredients, mixing well with apple mixture. Add chopped nuts. Spoon into a greased and floured stem pan. Bake at 350° for 1 hour. Cool briefly before removing from pan.

Makes 8-10 servings.

Mrs. John McNeely
Shreveport

Asparagus and Shrimp Salad

¾ lb. cooked shrimp
1 medium can green asparagus tips
1 small head lettuce
2 hard-boiled eggs, chopped
1 clove garlic
½ teaspoon salt
1 bottle French dressing (Lowery's Sherry French Dressing)

Cover shrimp with french dressing and marinate 1-2 hours. Drain. Rub salad bowl with clove of garlic. Break lettuce, add asparagus tips and toss thoroughly with dressing. Sprinkle with table salt. Arrange shrimp on top.

Makes 2-4 servings.

Mrs. Printis E. Murphy
Oakdale

Bean Salad

½ cup sugar
⅔ cup vinegar
⅓ cup salad oil
1 teaspoon salt
1 teaspoon black pepper
1 can cut green beans
1 can wax beans
1 can kidney beans (high quality)
1 can garbanzo beans
2 red onions (fresh, small, sliced)
1 cup chopped celery
1 bell pepper, chopped

Mix sugar, vinegar, salad oil, salt and black pepper. Drain all beans and combine with onions, celery and bell pepper. Mix vinegar mixture with bean mixture and let set out 1 or 2 hours before storing in refrigerator. Store at least overnight, but the salad keeps well for a long time refrigerated. You can cut down on the sugar.

Virginia Triche
LaPlace

Three Bean Salad

1 — 16 oz. can whole green beans
1 — 16 oz. can cut wax beans
1 — 16 oz. can red kidney beans
1 teaspoon salt
½ cup chopped onions
½ cup sugar
½ cup salad oil
½ cup Heinz salad vinegar

Drain all beans and rinse well with cold water. Cut green beans in half. Mix all other ingredients well and pour over beans. Put in refrigerator in a covered bowl overnight before serving. Keep in refrigerator.

NOTE: This is a pretty easy dish that can be made ahead of time and kept for days in refrigerator and it is good!

Mrs. S. P. Borden, Jr.
Shreveport

Candle-wick Salad

Pineapple slices
Bananas
Red Cherries
Lettuce leaves
Mayonnaise
Toothpicks

Place pineapple slices on lettuce. Cut bananas crosswise about two inches long. Place the banana end in the pineapple ring and and cherry on top of banana with a toothpick. Place mayonnaise o of banana to represent melting candle.

Marie
Lake F

Creamy Carrot Nut Mold

1 — 6 oz. package orange Jello
1 envelope unflavored gelatin
2 cups very hot water
1 cup thick sour cream
1 small Philadelphia cream cheese
1 — 15¼ oz. crushed pineapple (do not drain)
2 cups grated carrots
1 cup chopped nuts

Slightly grease mold; pour hot water over jello and gelatin and stir until dissolved. Gradually add gelatin to sour cream and cream cheese slowly stirring until well blended. Chill until mixture begins to jell. Stir in pineapple, carrots and nuts. Turn into mold and chill until firm. Unmold on lettuce leaves (optional).

Mary Jane Donaldson
Norco

Marinated Carrots

5 cups sliced carrots
1 small bell pepper
1 medium onion
½ cup salad oil
1 cup sugar
¾ cup vinegar
1 can tomato soup
1 teaspoon Worcestershire sauce
1 teaspoon each of mustard, salt and pepper

Cook carrots slightly and cool. Slice or chop pepper and onion. Put everything in bowl. Mix and marinate at least 12 hours.

Makes 8-10 servings.

NOTE: Keeps 2 weeks in refrigerator.

Miss Fleeta Howell
Lake Providence

Cauliflower and Broccoli

1 head cauliflower
1 bunch fresh croccoli
1 small onion, chopped

Dressing:
1 cup mayonnaise
1 tablespoon vinegar
Salt to taste

Break cauliflower into small pieces (discard stems). Break broccoli into tiny pieces. Mix cauliflower and broccoli with dressing and chill at least 2 hours or overnight before serving.

Makes 4 servings.

Mrs. T. A. Melancon
Mamou

Emerald Salad

1 — 8 oz. package cream cheese
1 — 8¼ oz. can crushed pineapple
1 — 3 oz. package lime jello
½ cup celery, finely chopped
½ cup pecans, finely chopped
½ cup mayonnaise

Drain pineapple and set aside. Dissolve jello in 1 cup boiling water. Use pineapple juice and water to make 2nd cup. Set mixture aside until it just starts to set firmly. Mix softened cream cheese, mayonnaise, nuts, celery and pineapple. Add this to jello and set until very firm.

Janice Beadle
Norco

Fruit Salad

1 can apricot pie filling
1 small package frozen strawberries, drained
1 large can crushed pineapple, drained
3 bananas, sliced

Mix ingredients together and store in covered container. Refrigerate.

NOTE: Also can be made with cherry pie filling, 1 can mandarin oranges and chopped pecans.

Mrs. A.H. (Winnie) Zackary, Sr.
Bossier City

Chicken Salad Royal

3 cups cooked cubed chicken breasts
1 cup sliced water chestnuts
2 cups pineapple tidbits, well drained
1 cup diced celery
½ cup onion, finely chopped
4 tablespoons Major Grey's chutney
1 cup sour cream
1 cup mayonnaise
1 teaspoon curry powder
1 can Chinese noodles

Mix chutney, sour cream, mayonnaise and curry powder. Add remaining ingredients except noodles. Mix and let stand overnight in refrigerator. Just before serving, mix in Chinese noodles.

Mrs. Robert Fenstermaker
Oakdale

Cucumber Salad

1 small package lime gelatin
1 cup boiling water
1 teaspoon salt
1 teaspoon grated onion
2 tablespoons vinegar
¼ cup chopped celery
¼ cup chopped green pepper
½ cup sour cream
1 cup grated cucumber
¼ cup mayonnaise

Dissolve gelatin in hot water. Add salt, onion and vinegar. Chill until almost set. Add remaining ingredients and chill until firm.

Doris D. Ledoux
DeRidder

Cucumber Lime Salad

1 package lime jello
1 cup hot water
2 — 3 oz. packages cream cheese
½ cup diced cucumber
1 small can crushed pineapple, drained
½ cup chopped pecans
½ cup mayonnaise
½ cup whipped cream
3 tablespoons chopped pimento

Dissolve jello in hot water. While jello is still hot, mix with cream cheese. Let mixture begin to congeal and then add remaining ingredients.

Makes 8 servings.

A friend from E. Carroll Parish

Lime Delight

1 small package lime jello
1 small package lemon jello
1 cup boiling water
1 large can crushed pineapple
¼ cup mayonnaise
¼ cup pecans
1 cup grated cheese
1 large Cool Whip

Dissolve both jellos in boiling water, add drained pineapple juice. Cool until first begins to jell, whip until foamy. Add pineapple, mayonnaise, pecans, cheese and ¾ of Cool Whip. Mix by hand and pour into pan. Cover with remaining Cool Whip.

Makes 12 servings.

Adelle Quinn
Wilson

Pickled English Pea Salad

1 can Petit-Pois peas
½ jar India Relish
1 cup dried celery
Mayonnaise

Drain peas the night before serving and place the India Relish on top. Next day add celery and enough mayonnaise to hold together. Serve on lettuce.

Makes 6 servings.

Mrs. Frank D'Autremont
LeCompte

Pea Bean Salad

1 cup mayonnaise
2 tablespoons capers
1 tablespoon liquid from capers
1 tablespoon minced onion
¼ teaspoon garlic powder
1 package Delaney tiny lima beans
1 — 17 oz. can LeSueur peas, drained
½ cup stuffed olives, sliced
½ cup sliced ripe olives

Mix together mayonnaise, capers, liquid, onion and garlic powder. Refrigerate for one to two hours. Cook lima beans according to instructions on the package. Drain. Add these to peas and olives. Fold in mayonnaise mixture. Refrigerate until ready to serve.

Makes 6 servings.

Winnie Raggio
Jonesboro

Golden Rice Salad

¼ cup salad oil
1½ teaspoons salt
⅛ teaspoon pepper
1 cup chopped ripe olives
2 hard boiled eggs
1½ cup chopped celery
1 cup chopped onion
¼ cup chopped pickles
½ cup mayonnaise
2 tablespoons mustard
2 tablespoons vinegar
⅛ teaspoon red pepper
4½ cups cooked rice (1½ cups raw rice cooked in 3 cups chicken broth)

Blend oil, vinegar, salt and pepper. Pour over hot cooked rice. Toss and set aside to cool. Add remaining ingredients; toss and chill thoroughly.

NOTE: Parsley and green onions may be added.

Mrs. Sybil Callender Ward
Sisterdale, Texas

Salmon Salad Piquant

1 tablespoon (1 envelope) unflavored gelatin
½ cup cold water
2 egg yolks, slightly beaten
¾ cup milk
½ teaspoon salt
1½ teaspoons prepared mustard
Dash of cayenne pepper
1½ tablespoons butter or margarine
½ cup lemon juice
1 — 7¾ oz. can salmon, flaked
Lettuce
Lemon slices
Cucumber cream dressing (see below)

Soften gelatin in cold water. Combine egg yolks, milk, salt, mustard and cayenne pepper in top of double boiler. Place over simmering water; cook until thickened (about 8 minutes) stirring constantly. Blend in butter and lemon juice. Add softened gelatin, stirring until dissolved. Remove from heat. Stir in salmon. Cool. Pour salmon mixture into an oiled 1 quart mold and chill until firm. Unmold on bed of lettuce and garnish with lemon slices. Serve with Cucumber Cream Dressing.

Cucumber Cream Dressing:

1 medium cucumber, peeled
2 tablespoons sugar
2 tablespoons vinegar
1 cup whipping cream, whipped

Cut cucumber in half lengthwise; remove seeds and discard. Cut cucumber into ¼-inch cubes; combine with sugar and vinegar, and fold in whipped cream. Chill. Yield: about 3 cups.

Mrs. Herman L. (Genevieve) Kelley, Jr.
Bunkie

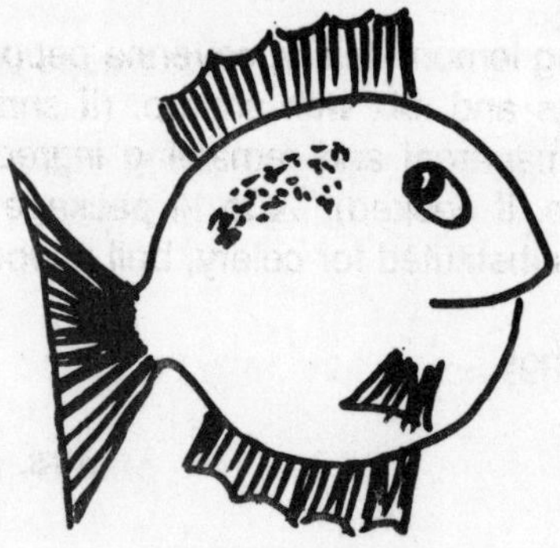

New Orleans Shrimp Salad

1 cup cooked rice
1 cup cooked, peeled shrimp
½ cup diced raw cauliflower
¼ cup minced onion
¼ cup chopped green onion
¼ cup chopped celery
4 stuffed olives, sliced
½ cup mayonnaise
¼ cup French dressing
½ teaspoon salt
1 tablespoon lemon juice
Lettuce leaves

Combine all ingredients except lettuce. Toss lightly. Chill thoroughly and serve on lettuce.

Makes 4 servings.

Hazel C. Gourgues
Hahnville

Shrimp and Shells

3 cups peeled, deveined, boiled shrimp
3 eggs, hard cooked and chopped
1½ cups cooked macaroni, shells or elbow
¼ cup chopped celery
¼ cup chopped bell pepper
¼ cup chopped onion
1 teaspoon chopped garlic
½ cup mayonnaise
2 tablespoons mustard
1 tablespoon lemon juice
Salt and pepper to taste (McCormick's Nature Seasoning may be substituted.)

Boil shrimp, using lemon, celery, cayenne pepper, salt and onion to taste. Chop eggs and mix with shrimp. (If shrimp are large, chop coarsely.) Add macaroni and remaining ingredients. Mix well and serve (on lettuce, if desired). ⅛ to ¼ package frozen Chef's Seasoning may be substituted for celery, bell pepper, onion and garlic.

Makes 6-8 servings.

Mrs. Frank (Mary) Daviet
Lockport

Salad Louise

1 bag spinach or romaine
1 can Chinese noodles (Chow Mein)
1 can bean sprouts, crisped
1 can water chestnuts
4 hard cooked eggs, chopped
½ lb. bacon, crisp

Dressing:

⅓ cup vinegar
1 teaspoon salt
¾ cup sugar
1 teaspoon steak sauce
1 large onion, sliced thin
1 cup corn oil
(Let dressing stand overnight before using)

Blend dressing until creamy. Pour over salad ingredients which have been tossed together.

Makes 4 servings.

Mabel Reeves
Slidell

Spinach Salad

1 red onion
1 bag fresh spinach
½ lb. bacon
2 hard boiled eggs
¼ cup vinegar
¼ cup sugar
1 cup Miracle Whip salad dressing or mayonnaise
½ cup milk

Combine onion, sliced very thin; spinach, washed and cut up; bacon, diced and fried and drained; and diced eggs. Cream last 4 items together and pour over first 4 items.

Makes 10 servings.

Grady Loomis
LaPlace

Strawberry Nut Salad

2 small packages strawberry jello
1 cup boiling water
2 — 10 oz. frozen strawberries, thawed
1 can (1 lb. 4 oz.) crushed pineapple
1 cup coarsely chopped pecans
2 cartons sour cream

Dissolve jello in water. Add strawberries with juice, drained pineapple and nuts. Pour half of mixture in pyrex dish, refrigerate until firm. When congealed, spread sour cream over top. Then pour balance of mixture over all. Return to refrigerator until firm.
Makes 8 servings.

Mrs. Robert Fenstermaker
Oakdale

Water Gate Salad

1 — 20 oz. can crushed pineapple
1 package pistachio pudding (3¾ oz.)
1½ cups miniature marshmallows
½ cup chopped pecans
1 carton Cool Whip (9 ozs.)

Do not drain pineapple. Thaw Cool Whip. Mix all ingredients well. Put in a greased square or oblong container (9×9 or 8×12") and freeze. Cut in squares. May be served on lettuce leaf.

Not necessary to freeze — serve from bowl.

Marie S. Cook
Wilson

Cucumber Salad Dressing

3 medium cucumbers
¼ cup sugar
¼ cup lemon juice
1 quart mayonnaise
¼ teaspoon garlic powder
3 small onions
2 tablespoons Worcestershire sauce
¼ teaspoon green food coloring
¼ teaspoon monosodium glutamate

Grind onions and cucumbers. Put in colander and drain well. Add rest of ingredients and mix well. Keep in refrigerator in tightly covered container. Variation: Only 1 pint of mayonnaise can be used and add ¼ teaspoon Accent instead of monosodium glutamate.

NOTE: Delicious on tossed green salads.

Mrs. Jimmy Presley
Shreveport

Soups

Western Chile Soup

1½ lbs. ground beef
1 cup chopped onion
2 medium cloves garlic, minced
1 can Campbell's Beef Broth
2 cans (10¾ ozs. each) Campbell's Tomato Soup
1 soup can water
2 cans (15½ ozs. each) kidney beans, undrained
3 cups cooked elbow macaroni
3 tablespoons chile powder
2 tablespoons vinegar

In large heavy pan, brown beef and cook onion with garlic until tender. Stir to separate meat. Add remaining ingredients. Simmer 30 minutes, stirring occasionally.

Makes 12 servings.

NOTE: Great with hot cornbread!

Carol Rushing
Farmerville

Corn Soup

1 lb. ham chunks
3 fresh tomatoes
2 cups chopped onion
2 toes chopped garlic
2 stalks sliced celery
2 cans corn
2 teaspoons salt
¼ teaspoon pepper
8 ears yellow corn
2 quarts water

Combine all ingredients except fresh corn in a soup pot. Bring to a boil, then simmer. While this is simmering, cut very top of fresh kernel of corn from cob, then use back of knife to remove milk from cob. Add corn and corn milk to soup. Cook one hour.

Makes 6-8 servings.

NOTE: I usually cut 2 of the ears of corn in thirds and add these pieces to the soup for added flavor.

Caroline Webster Derbes
Luling

Gazpacho Adams Style

1 — 5½ oz. Snap-E-Tom
2 — 14½ oz. cans sliced tomatoes
1 medium bell pepper, chopped
5¾ ozs. pitted black olives, sliced thin
¾ cup chopped celery
¾ cup chopped green onions
¾ cup chopped cucumber (seedless if available)
¾ cup Chablis wine
2 cloves garlic, chopped
3 tablespoons red wine vinegar
3 bouillon cubes, dissolved in water
1 teaspoon Worcestershire
6 drops Tabasco sauce
1 — 10½ oz. can condensed beef broth
Chives, chopped
Croutons

Pour Snap-E-Tom in large bowl. Drain juice from tomatoes into this bowl, and set the tomatoes aside. Place vinegar, Worcestershire sauce, bouillon, Tabasco, beef broth and wine in blender. Add celery, onion and garlic; blend on *chop.* After chopped fine, add to Snap-E-Tom and tomato juice in large bowl. Chop cucumber in the blender for only a few seconds and add to bowl. Add the olives. Chop sliced tomatoes in large pieces and add to bowl. Chill 24 hours. This is important to the flavor. Ladle into *CHILLED* soup bowls. Garnish with chives and croutons.

Makes a little over two quarts, which is 6-8 servings.

Alex Adams II
Ruston

Shrimp Okra Gumbo

2 medium sized onions, chopped
3 lbs. shrimp
2 lbs. okra
1 gallon hot water
½ clove garlic
2 tablespoons oil or shortening

Fry onion until brown around edges. Add peeled shrimp and okra sliced in rounds ⅛ inch thick. Cook over *simmer flame,* stirring occasionally for about 1 hour. When okra ceases to "rope", add slowly 1 cup hot water every few minutes. Cover and continue to simmer for another hour. Season to taste. Serve with rice.

Makes 8 servings.

NOTE: This freezes very well!

Mrs. Fred G. Anepohl, Jr.
Baton Rouge

Okra Gumbo

½ cup oil
3 lbs. okra
1 lb. shrimp
5 crabs broken in half
1 small pack ham seasoning
1 cup onion
½ bell pepper
3 toes garlic
1 can tomatoes
1 can tomato paste
1 tablespoon parsley
1 teaspoon salt and pepper
1 teaspoon Seasoning All
2 teaspoons gumbo file'
3 bay leaves
½ teaspoon thyme
4 or 5 cups water

In one big skillet, fry okra until dry of slime — don't use oil, just dry skillet. In another pot put ½ cup of oil in pot; make sure pot is warn, and simmer onion, garlic, bell pepper, and parsley for 15 minutes. Add shrimp and ham seasoning and simmer 15 more minutes. Next add tomatoes, tomatoe paste, salt, pepper, Seasoning All, file', bay leaf, thyme, parsley and water. Add more water when necessary. Cook until done. Serve over steamed rice.

Makes 12 servings.

Stella L. Bradix Thomas
Algiers

Chicken Gumbo

1 large fryer, cut-up
1 bell pepper (large), chopped
1 large onion, chopped
⅛ teaspoon garlic powder or two bottons garlic, minced
3 bay leaves
½ lb. link smoked sausage, sliced
¼ cup bacon drippings
⅓-½ cup all-purpose flour
2 tablespoons gumbo file'

Cook chicken in 4-quart container (preferably iron pot). Bring to boil, reduce to simmer. Add bell pepper, onion, garlic, whole bay leaves and sausage rounds. Simmer until chicken is tender. Remove chicken from broth, cool and debone and remove skin. Return to broth.

Roux: Brown flour in ¼ cup bacon drippings very slowly (at least 30-40 minutes). Add roux to chicken. Simmer on very low heat until almost serving time. Remove from heat. Add approximately 2 tablespoons gumbo file'. (Do not boil after file' has been added.) File' can be served at table if stronger taste is desired. Serve over steamed rice with crackers.

Makes 6-8 servings.

NOTE: Sliced okra can be used in gumbo if desired. I personally don't use it.

Azalea Hudnall
Jena

Chicken Gumbo

Roux: 2 tablespoons flour and 2 tablespoons oil
Approximately 3½ lbs. chicken (12 chicken thighs — skin removed)
1½ lbs. Hormel Smoked Sausage (cut in serving pieces) or 1½ lbs. undooey sausage OR BOTH

2 quarts water
3 tablespoons Worcestershire sauce
1 tablespoon salt (add more if needed later)
Pepper to taste
½ cup shallots
Parsley to taste
2 medium onions
2 tablespoons flour
1 tablespoon File' seasoning
1-1½ cups okra (optional)

Advance preparation: remove all skin from chicken. Boil smoked sausage for ½ hour to remove oil from sausage (not mandatory). Cut sausage into serving pieces. Chop shallots, parsley and onions. You can begin with a roux (browned flour) and add shallots, onions, parsley, seasoning, and water. Add chicken after that OR you can also cook as follows: put water on to boil, add Worcestershire sauce, place chicken and sausage in water. Add all other ingredients except flour and file'. The onions, etc. will cook down in the gravy and become tender without having to fry them in a roux. After chicken becomes tender from cooking on medium heat — covered — (approx. 1 to 1½ hours) — be sure chicken is tender — then add flour to ½ cup HOT water and mix well. Strain the flour and water mixture into gravy and stir quickly as it can become lumpy. Add File' and cook about another ½ hour with NO cover and gumbo is ready to eat. If you like it a little thicker, add a little more flour. But cooking it without the cover will usually thicken it enough. Skim off excess fat.

Joan Folse
Luling

Split Pea Potage

½ lb. split peas
1 small Irish potato cut in ½ inch cubes
½ small onion, cut in quarters
Ham hock (or 5 or 6 pieces of ham cut in cubes)
5 cups water
1½ tablespoons tomato catsup
1 tablespoon Worcestershire sauce

Rinse split peas and drain. Place above ingredients in boiler, cook for about 30 minutes and then season to taste with salt, pepper, and seasoning salt or garlic salt (cooking for 30 minutes allows you to see how salty ham is before seasoning). Cook over low heat stirring frequently for 1 hour until peas are mushy. If too thick, add water. Fifteen minutes before removing from heat, add tomato catsup and Worcestershire sauce. Serve with pieces of ham in each bowl.

Makes 6 servings.

Mrs. Leroy Vogel
Shreveport

Dot's Squash Bisque

Saute 1 medium onion (chopped) with 2 tablespoons oleo (or butter) until tender

Add:

1 quart chicken broth (canned or your own)
4 cups yellow squash cut in large pieces (or use zucchini)
¾ cup carrots, cut up
½ teaspoon thyme
Salt and pepper to taste

Simmer above until just tender, then in blender: blend the above and add either 1 large can of evaporated milk or 1 cup half and half. Serve warm in cups or bowls. May add parsley for garnish.

Mrs. W. B. Liles
Monroe

On The Shelf

Fresh Sweet Pickles

4 medium size cucumbers, thinly sliced — sprinkle with salt and allow to set for several hours (2-3). DRAIN. *DO NOT WASH.*

In large glass or plastic bowl combine:
2 cups sugar
1 cup cider vinegar
1 tablespoon celery seed
Stir to dissolve sugar

Add:
2 large onions, thinly sliced
1 green pepper, thinly sliced

Add drained cucumbers and mix well. Marinate several hours or overnight. Keep refrigerated.

NOTE: Will keep for several weeks.

Makes 6 servings.

Doris D. Ledoux
DeRidder

Ice Cream Salt Pickles

Cucumbers, small to medium size
6 quarts water
4 cups white Surfine vinegar
2 cups ice cream salt
Fresh dill

Wash cucumbers and drain well. Wash and scald quart jars. Put a head or flower of fresh dill on bottom of jar. Pack whole cucumbers or slice thin to use for hamburger style pickles. In large pan boil water, vinegar and salt till salt is dissolved. Pour boiling solution over cucumbers and seal each jar immediately with hot seals. If you have plenty of dill you can lay a head on top of cucumbers in each jar.

Makes 13-14 quarts

Mrs. Jimmy Presley
Shreveport

Red Cinnamon Pickles

2 gallons cucumber rings
2 cups lime
8½ quarts water
1 cup vinegar
1 — 10 oz. bottle red food coloring
1 tablespoon alum
3 cups white vinegar
3 cups water
30 ozs. red hots
15 cups sugar
12 sticks cinnamon

Use very large cucumbers which are beginning to turn yellow or white. Peel, cut into rings ½ inch thick and remove seeds. Mix lime and 8½ quarts water well. Pour over rings and let stand 24 hours. Drain and carefully wash through several waters and let stand in ice water for 3 hours. Drain, cover with 1 cup vinegar, food coloring and alum. Add enough water to cover and simmer for 3 hours; drain on thick towels. In large pan make a syrup of 3 cups vinegar, 3 cups water, cinnamon, red hots and sugar. Heat until sugar and red hots are dissolved. Put rings in large pan or bowl and pour boiling solution over them. Every day for three days drain off syrup, reheat and pour back over cucumbers. On the fourth day reheat syrup. Pack rings in large mouth quart or pint jars and pour boiling syrup into jars. Seal each jar immediately. Continue till all jars are filled. They are ready to use anytime.

Mrs. Jimmy Presley
Shreveport

Pimientos

14-15 large red bell peppers
1 tablespoon special canning salt
1 tablespoon dry mustard
2 tablespoons butter (not oleo)
½ cup sugar
2 tablespoons flour
1 cup white vinegar
½ of pepper juice

Wash, core and drain peppers. Set up food grinder. Set clean bowl on floor under grinder to catch juice to save. Set another bowl under grinder and grind peppers. In large pan or kettle add pepper. In bowl mix salt, flour, dry mustard and sugar. Add vinegar and small amount of pepper juice to make thin paste, and add to peppers, then add ½ of pepper juice. Bring to a boil and cook 5 minutes. Fill sterilized ½ pint (or baby food size jar, baby juice jars are perfect). Seal each immediately with hot seals. Set on seal ends. Ready to use.

NOTE: After you use this you won't ever go back to regular pimientos.

Mrs. Jimmy Presley
Shreveport

Baked, Frozen Sweet Potatoes

1 bushel sweet potatoes
Ice water
6-8 lemons (squeezed)
Lemon rind
Sugar, granulated (white)
Butter

Wash amount of potatoes you want to put in freezer. (Usually 1 bushel.) Put in large pan and cover with warm water. Put lid or foil over the top and punch small holes for steam. Cook till tender and jackets will slip off. Take out of water. As soon as you can handle, take off peel. Drop peeled potatoes in large pot full of ice water and about 6-8 lemons squeezed (do not use juice, just pulp) and add lemon rind. Let potatoes set till completely cold. Lay potatoes out on heavy thick towels to drain. Have foil cake pans ready. Roll dried potatoes in granulated sugar and lay in pans. If potato is too large, cut in half and then roll in sugar. Continue this till all potatoes are in pans. Cover with foil. Put in freezer. When ready to use set out to thaw. Slit each potato and add pieces of butter. Sprinkle on more sugar, put in oven at 300° and cook 30 minutes to 1 hour.

Mrs. Jimmy Presley
Shreveport

Bring-A-Dish

Chicken and Broccoli

2 packages frozen broccoli
3 chicken breasts
1 can cream of chicken soup
1 cup mayonnaise
2 tablespoons onion, chopped
2 tablespoons lemon juice
½ teaspoon curry powder
Salt to taste
Pepper to taste
1 cup cheddar cheese, grated
Paprika
Cheese or Ritz cracker crumbs

Cook broccoli according to package directions. Boil chicken breasts (with a little onion and celery added to water for seasoning) until done. Place chopped broccoli and chicken breasts in a buttered casserole dish. Mix cream of chicken soup with 1 cup mayonnaise and add to chicken. Add onion, lemon juice, curry powder, salt and pepper and mix well. Spread grated cheese on top and sprinkle with paprika and cracker crumbs.

Callie Jones
Coushatta

Chicken Casserole

1 — 8 oz. package Pepperidge Farm Cornbread Dressing
1½ lb. stick margarine
2 — 10¾ oz. cans cream of chicken soup
4 large chicken breasts or 1 whole chicken

Stew chicken without salt. Pick off bones, save broth. Melt margarine and stir in dressing (save some dressing mix, dry, for topping). Dilute cream of chicken soup with 1 to 2 cups of broth. Grease 13×9 inch dish. Put a layer of dressing, layer of chicken, layer of chicken soup. Repeat process. Top with crumbs. Bake at 350° until brown, approximately 45 minutes to 1 hour.

Makes 6-8 servings.

Mrs. Joe Ann Brown
West Monroe

Chicken Casserole

1 — 4-5 lb. chicken
1 cup chopped celery
1 cup chopped onion
1 cup chopped green pepper
½ cup melted oleo
1 — 8 oz. package spinach noodles
1 — 4 oz. can mushrooms
1 cup chopped stuffed olives
1 — 10¾ oz. can cream of celery or mushroom soup
1 lb. cheddar cheese, shredded
1 cup cracker crumbs

Cook chicken. Drain, reserving liquid broth. Debone and cut in small pieces. Saute celery, onions and green peppers in oleo. Cook noodles in broth until done. Drain. Combine all ingredients except cracker crumbs, mixing gently. Spoon into 4 quart casserole and top with cracker crumbs. Bake at 350° for 1 hour.

Makes 12 servings.

Mrs. Coan Knight
Leesville

Chicken Casserole

1 fryer, boiled and boned
½ cup broth
1 tablespoon chili powder
½ teaspoon garlic powder
1 onion, chopped
1 bell pepper, chopped
1 Jalapeno pepper, chopped
1 can cream of mushroom soup
1 can cream of chicken soup
1 can Rotel tomatoes
1 cup grated cheese
1 large package Dorito chips

Mix first 10 ingredients together (you may freeze or store in refrigerator at this stage). In casserole dish add a layer of dorito chips, a layer of the chicken mix — a layer of dorito chips and the rest of the chicken mix. Put cheese on top. Bake in moderate oven until cheese is brown.

Mrs. Beth Smith
Winnfield

Stacked Enchilades Chicken

6 large or 10 small corn tortillas
2½ cups grated cheese (6 ozs.)
1 — 10 oz. can enchilada sauce filling
2 cups cooked chopped chicken
1 cup sour cream
¼ cup chopped green onions, (including tops)
½ teaspoon salt
¼ teaspoon cumin

For filling, combine sour cream, chicken, onions, salt and cumin. Mix well. Dip tortillas in enchilada sauce. Place one tortilla in a 1½ quart casserole dish. Top with 4 tablespoons chicken filling and spread over tortilla. Sprinkle with ⅓ cup grated cheese. Repeat layers of tortilla, filling and cheese. Before adding last layer of cheese, pour remaining enchilada sauce over all. Top with cheese. Bake at 350° for 40 minutes.

Makes 6 servings.

Mrs. Mae Machen
Jonesboro

Chicken Escort

2 packages chicken breasts or 1 — 3½ lb. chicken
1 — 10½ oz. can cream of chicken soup
1 — 10½ oz. can cream of mushroom soup
1 cup sour cream
1 box Escort crackers
1 small jar of pimento

Boil chicken in salty water until done. Cool, debone and cut into small pieces. Heat undiluted soups until blended and remove from heat. Fold in sour cream. Add chicken to mixture. Crush Escort crackers and cover bottom of 2-quart oblong Pyrex dish which has been sprayed with Pam. Add layer of chicken mixture and cover with cracker crumbs. Alternate layers if making a larger casserole. *CAUTION* — too many cracker crumbs will result in dryness. Pimento may be added for color. Bake in 350° oven about 30 minutes or until bubbly.

Makes 8 servings.

Mrs. J. G. Key
Jonesboro

Chicken Italiano

1 — 2-3 lb. chicken, cut up
1 — 28 oz. can Italian tomatoes
¼ cup olive oil
1 or 2 cloves garlic, minced
2-3 sprigs parsley, chopped
1½ teaspoons salt
¾ teaspoon whole oregano
¾ teaspoon whole basil
¼ teaspoon crushed red pepper
¼ teaspoon pepper
¼ cup grated parmesan cheese
Hot cooked spaghetti

Place chicken pieces, skin side up, in a 13×9×2 inch baking pan. Set chicken aside. Drain tomatoes, reserving liquid; chop tomatoes. Combine tomatoes, tomato liquid, olive oil, garlic, parsley and seasonings; stir well. Pour tomato mixture over chicken and bake at 375° for 1 hour. Turn chicken, sprinkle with cheese, and bake an additional 45 minutes to one hour. Serve over spaghetti.

Makes 6 servings.

NOTE: May be prepared day before, deboned, then reheated and served over spaghetti later. May also be frozen without spaghetti.

Mrs. Jerome (Linda) Alesi
Lafayette

Mexican Chicken

1 — 2½-3 lb. chicken
2 ribs celery, chopped
2 onions, chopped
1 bell pepper, chopped
1 — 8 oz. package tortilla chips, broken
2 tablespoons oleo
1 — 10¾ oz. can mushroom soup
1 — 10¾ oz. can chicken soup
1 — 10 oz. can Rotel tomatoes
1½ cups shredded cheese
¾ cup chicken broth

Cook chicken in salted water. Save broth and debone chicken. Cut up and set aside. Saute onions, pepper and celery in oleo. Add soups and Rotel to this. Mix in chicken. In 9¾×9¾×2″ casserole dish put layer of chicken mixture, layer of chips and cheese. Keep repeating until all is used. Put some cheese on top. Pour ¾ cup of chicken broth on top of this. Sprinkle chili powder on top if desired. Bake at 350° for 40-45 minutes.

Makes 6 servings.

Helen Wilson
Delhi

Chicken in Foil

1 large whole uncooked chicken breast
2 or 3 scallions (or onion in small slices)
2 slices fresh ginger root (or ½ teaspoon ginger)
1 tablespoon dry sherry (or Sauterne)
1 tablespoon soy sauce
½ teaspoon salt
½ teaspoon sugar
20 squares 6×6″ foil (fold into 3-corner envelope)
2 cups vegetable oil for deep frying

Skin and debone chicken breast. Cut into 20 slices about 1×1×1½″ Marinate chicken in 1 tablespoon sherry, 1 tablespoon soy sauce, ½ teaspoon salt, ½ teaspoon sugar, ginger and onions for 20 minutes. Grease foil squares with a drop of oil. Place 1 piece of chicken and a piece of onion in each with about a spoonful of marinade, and wrap in 3-corner shape. Tuck in flaps carefully to complete the envelope. Heat 2 cups oil to 370°. Deep fry packages a few at a time on *flap side up* for 2-3 minutes. Turn over and fry a few seconds more. Drain and serve hot. Makes 20 packages.

Mattie Somerville
Monroe

Chicken Tetrazini

1 hen or large fryer
Salt to taste
Pepper to taste
1 package spaghetti
4 cans mushroom soup
1 can sliced water chestnuts
1 cup grated cheese
2 medium size bell peppers, chopped
1 cup chopped celery
4 garlic cloves, minced
4 medium onions, chopped
6 tablespoons oil

Boil chicken till tender. Cut into chunks. Cook spaghetti in boiling broth until tender. Chop together celery, peppers, onions and garlic. Tenderize in oil. Add to spaghetti. Add chopped chicken and mushroom soup. Add water chestnuts, salt and pepper to taste. Pour into casserole. Cover with grated cheese. Bake in moderate oven 30-40 minutes.

Makes 8-10 servings with seconds.

NOTE: Flavor improved when served second day.

Mrs. Ben F. Post
Farmerville

Chicken Treasure

4 whole chicken breasts
⅓ cup butter
½ cup flour
1 teaspoon salt
1 cup milk
2 cups chicken broth
1 teaspoon lemon juice
1 cup mayonnaise
2 — 15 oz. cans asparagus
½ cup toasted bread crumbs

Simmer chicken in boiling water salted to cover for 1 hour or until tender. Save 2 cups broth. Spread chicken on plate to cool. Debone. Remove fat and skin — cut chicken into bite size pieces. Melt butter, stir in flour and salt. Add milk and broth. Cook until creamy and thick, stirring constantly. Beat lemon juice and mayonnaise together and stir into creamy sauce. Remove from heat and stir well. Lightly grease 2½-quart casserole dish and layer chicken and asparagus alternately. Pour sauce over and top with bread crumbs. Bake at 375° for 45 minutes or until bubbly.

Makes 6-8 servings.

Jackie Burroughs
Shreveport

Seafood Jambalaya

4 tablespoons flour
4 tablespoons oil
1 large onion, chopped
1 large bell pepper, chopped
1 lb. shrimp
1 — 8 oz. can tomato sauce
½ teaspoon seafood seasoning
1 teaspoon garlic powder
2 bay leaves
Salt and pepper to taste
1 lb. crab meat
1 teaspoon chopped parsley
4 cups cooked rice

Make roux. Simmer onions and bell pepper in roux. Add shrimp, simmer until juice is out of shrimp, add tomato sauce, seafood seasoning, arlic powder, bay leaves, salt and pepper to taste. Simmer about 30 minutes, add crab meat and parsley. Simmer another 30 minutes. Simmer with lid on pot. Add cooked rice. Simmer about 5 minutes more and turn off heat and let stand awhile before serving.

Makes 8 servings.

Mrs. Olie Adams
Thibodaux

Jambalaya

1 fryer, about 2½ lbs.
1 lb. smoked sausage
1 medium onion
1 stalk celery
¼ medium bell pepper
1 toe garlic
2 teaspoons salt
1½ teaspoon chili powder
½ teaspoon thyme
3 cups chicken stock
1 cup water
2 cups washed, uncooked rice

Cook and debone chicken in 3 cups water. In a blender put 1 cup water with onion, celery, bell pepper and garlic. Blend until vegetables are dissolved. In a dutch oven put chicken, sausage, and vegetables from blender with water, all seasonings and chicken stock making sure there are 3 cups (adding water if you have to). Cook for 10 minutes. Add washed rice, put lid on dutch oven, and bake in preheated oven at 400° for 35-40 minutes or until rice is done. After baking 20 minutes, stir rice to mix meat with rice. Cook until done.

Paul Loup
Bridge City

Jambalaya

1 lb. shelled and deveined shrimp
2 small eggplants, peeled and cubed
Salt and pepper to taste
2 teaspoons lemon juice
¼ teaspoon Tabasco sauce
3 tablespoons cooking oil
3 tablespoons flour
1 cup chopped onion
½ cup chopped green pepper
½ cup chopped celery
2 cups water
1 cup long grain rice, raw
1 teaspoon leaf oregano
2 teaspoons parsley flakes

Place shrimp and eggplant into a bowl, adding salt and pepper to taste, and mix well. Stir the lemon juice and Tabasco together and drizzle over mixture. In a heavy pan or dutch oven preheat cooking oil over medium heat. Then add flour, blending well and stirring occasionally until medium brown. Add onion, green pepper, and celery and saute just until wilted. Pour in the water, shrimp and eggplant. Sprinkle rice evenly over all, and then the oregano and parsley flakes. Cover pan; place asbestos plate under it and cook over low heat for 30 minutes, or until done.

Makes 6-8 servings.

NOTE: This dish can be made ahead of time and refrigerated, or frozen in a container suitable for stove top, or oven warming.

Mrs. Philip Zaunbrecher
Hayes

Sausage Jambalaya

2 lbs. pork link sausages
3 tablespoons bacon drippings
1 onion, chopped
2 ribs of celery, chopped
½ bell pepper, chopped fine
2 cups rice
4 cups water
Salt to taste
Pepper to taste

Brown sausage in bacon drippings. Saute celery, onion and bell pepper in same drippings until light brown, being careful not to burn. Brown rice until light brown — do not burn. Drain rice from drippings when brown. In heavy pot cook rice, 4 cups water, sausage, celery, onion, garlic and bell pepper. Bring to a boil, reduce heat to lowest point and cook 20-30 minutes.

Makes 10 servings.

NOTE: You may add green onion and 2 tablespoons of parsley.

Dorothy McGraw
Jackson

Cheddar Beef Pie

1 lb. ground beef
1 egg
⅓ cup chopped onion
¾ cup corn flake crumbs
1 tablespoon salt
Dash of pepper
2 tablespoons barbeque sauce
½ cup celery slices
2 tablespoons margarine
1 — 4 oz. can mushrooms, drained
¼ cup corn flake crumbs
1½ cups shredded cheddar cheese

Combine meat, egg, onion, corn flake crumbs (¾ cup), seasonings and barbeque sauce. Mix lightly. Press meat mixture onto bottom and sides of 9″ pie plate. Bake at 400° for 15 minutes. Remove meat shell from oven, drain. Reduce oven temperature to 350°. Saute celery slices in 1 tablespoon margarine. Combine celery, cheese and mushrooms. Toss lightly; spoon into hot meat shell. Melt remaining margarine and combine with ¼ cup crumbs; sprinkle over cheese mixture. Return to oven, continue baking 10 minutes.

Makes 6 servings.

Denise Humphreys
Luling

Godfather Meatloaf

2 lbs. ground meat
¾ cup Italian bread crumbs
1 cup Rotel chili tomatoes
2 eggs
Garlic
Salt
Pepper
2 thin slices ham
3 slices mozzarella cheese
1 small jar Ragu spaghetti sauce

Mix first seven (7) ingredients and flatten out ground meat mixture on wax paper. Put one layer of ham and one layer (2 slices) of mozzarella cheese in center. Fold each end over and make seam. Turn seam down in baking dish. Drain grease off after cooking 20 minutes at 350°. Cook until done. Add slice of mozzarella cheese and Ragu sauce to top and cook 15 minutes more.

Makes 10 servings.

Mrs. Elwanda P. Harvey
Leesville

Green Enchiladas

1 dozen flour tortillas
1½ lbs. hamburger meat
2 lbs. grated Velveeta cheese
1 can green chilies, chopped (6 may be enough)
1 can cream of chicken soup
1 — 12 oz. can evaporated milk
1 large onion, chopped

In 9×13 inch pan, well greased and sprayed with Pam, line the bottom with tortillas (use from the package with no prior preparation). Spread half of browned hamburger over tortillas, then half of grated cheese over meat. Repeat second layer with rest of tortillas, meat and cheese. Mix last four ingredients and pour over the above. Cover with foil and bake at 375° for 1½ hours.

NOTE: Can be prepared several hours or a day in advance. Refrigerate. Just before baking pour sauce over mix.

Charlotte Morrison
Alexandria

Italian Spaghetti

1½ lbs. lean ground beef
1 onion, chopped
1 — 16 oz. can tomatoes
1 — 6 oz. can tomato paste
2 — 8 oz. cans tomato sauce
3 cups water
1 small bell pepper, chopped
16 ozs. spaghetti
¼ cup wine vinegar
1 teaspoon salt
½ teaspoon pepper
1 teaspoon garlic salt
1 teaspoon Italian seasoning
½ teaspoon oregano
1 bay leaf

Brown ground beef with onion and bell pepper. Combine remaining ingredients, except spaghetti, and add meat. Simmer on low fire for 3 hours. Serve over cooked spaghetti. Top with parmesan cheese. Makes 6 servings.

NOTE: This stores better when sauce and spaghetti are put into separate containers.

Debbie Coplen
Farmerville

Meat Balls and Sauce

Meat Balls:

1 lb. ground meat
¼ lb. sausage
1 tablespoon parsley flakes
1 large onion, chopped fine
1 clove garlic, chopped fine
½ loaf French bread, shredded
1½ teaspoon salt
Pepper to taste

Meat Sauce:

2 tablespoons parsley flakes
1 tablespoon Mexican chili powder
½ cup beef broth
2 tablespoons bacon drippings
1 quart can tomatoes
1 can tomato sauce
1 large onion, chopped
1 clove garlic, chopped
½ cup celery, chopped

Meat Balls: Mix together all meat ball ingredients. Form into balls, brown in small amount of oil and drain on paper towels.

Meat Sauce: Simmer all of the ingredients 1 hour in large Dutch oven. Add the meat balls and simmer at least 30 minutes. This may be served over spaghetti or rice.

Makes 6-8 servings.

NOTE: Can be used as an appetizer.

Joyce Hunter
Delhi

Mini Meatballs and Spaghetti

½ cup chopped onion
½ cup chopped bell pepper
2 pods garlic, chopped
1 lb. ground beef
Dash of salt
¼ teaspoon black pepper
1 teaspoon Accent
1 egg
2 tablespoons flour
2 teaspoons chili powder
1 — 12 oz. package spaghetti
1 — 12 oz. can tomato paste

Cook spaghetti and leave in water. Combine all remaining ingredients except tomato paste. Shape into miniature meatballs. Fry in deep fat until slightly brown on both sides. Drain spaghetti. Add mini meatballs to spaghetti, along with tomato paste. Let simmer on low heat for about 20 minutes.

Makes 6-8 servings.

Charleen Jones
Jena

Rice Balls

3 lbs. ground round or lean beef
3 lbs. short grain rice
2 small cans tomato sauce
1 cup bread crumbs
3 tablespoons oil
Salt and pepper to taste
1 stick oleo
4 medium onions, chopped fine
6 eggs
7 stalks celery, chopped
Chili powder to taste
(about 2 tablespoons)

Brown meat in oil, saute onions and celery in oleo; add to meat mixture. Add tomato sauce, salt and pepper and cook slowly for about an hour; add chili powder, stirring occasionally. Cook rice until gummy, add oleo to rice, stirring until mixed well, set aside to cool. Beat eggs well. Moisten hands and make rice pattie about 4" square, place big heaping tablespoon meat mixture in rice cup (in hand) and seal edges over meat mixture. Dip in eggs, then in bread crumbs and place on cookie sheet. Fry in hot oil until golden brown.

Makes 3-4 dozen.

NOTE: Rice balls may be frozen, but thaw at room temperature before frying.

Louise W. Talley
Leesville

Beef Roll

1 round steak, cut ½" thick (flatten with meat pounder)
¼ cup olive oil
½ cup chopped green peppers
½ cup chopped celery
2 cloves garlic, minced
1 slice boiled ham, chopped
1 cup bread crumbs (any kind)
⅓ cup grated romano cheese
1 egg
2 slices bacon
1 cup sauterne wine

Salt and pepper the steak on both sides. Then heat the olive oil and fry the peppers, celery and garlic on a low flame; when mushy add the ham, bread crumbs and cook until golden brown. Then pour into a bowl and add the cheese and mix altogether with the egg; then spread the mixture on the steak, roll the steak and secure with string. Roll the bacon around the steak and bake 350° for 2 hours. The last 20 minutes add the wine. This makes a delicious gravy. When the steak is cool, slice and pour the gravy on it. Be sure you bake with a cover.

Mrs. Nada Natali
Iowa

Stuffed Beef Log

2 lbs. ground beef
½ cup quick-cooking oats, uncooked
½ cup finely chopped onion
½ cup milk
1 egg, beaten
2 teaspoons pepper
½ lb. mildly seasoned bulk sausage
1 medium potato, peeled and grated
1 cup bread crumbs
1 egg, beaten
¼ cup finely chopped onion
½ teaspoon salt

Combine first 7 ingredients; mix well. Shape into a 16×10" rectangle on aluminum foil or waxed paper. Combine the remaining ingredients; spread evenly over beef mixture. Roll jelly-roll fashion, beginning at short side, lifting paper to help roll. Place seam side down on a shallow baking pan. Bake at 300° for 1 hour and 30 minutes.

Makes 10-12 servings.

Mrs. Pat Painter
Lake Charles

Stuffed Flank Steak

1 flank steak
1 cup finely chopped onion
½ cup chopped carrot
½ cup chopped celery
4 tablespoons butter
1 cup cooked rice
1 egg, well beaten
1 small clove garlic, crushed
Salt and pepper to taste
½ cup red wine

Spread steak out flat and cut off any excess fat. Cook onion, carrots and celery slowly in 3 tablespoons butter in a deep heavy saucepan until soft but not browned. Put 1 cup of rice in large mixing bowl. Add cooked vegetables, egg and garlic. Season with salt and pepper. Blend and spread about half the stuffing on the steak, leaving a 1″ margin all around. Roll up lengthwise and tie with string at 2″ intervals. Heat 1 tablespoon butter in same pan as vegetables were cooked and when it is at the point of turning color, quickly brown the meat all over. Put balance of vegetables in pan and lightly brown them. Add wine and cook covered in a 350° oven for 2 hours.

To serve: Remove meat and cut off strings. Cut steak into slices. Arrange them slightly overlapping on a hot serving dish and surround with the vegetables.

Mrs. Bill Fuller
Kinder

Mama's Beef with Rusty Gravy

6 beef chops
½ teaspoonful salt
Dash black pepper
1 can tomato sauce
¼ cup Crisco shortening
3 tablespoonfuls flour

Brown beef chops in Crisco. Take out chops and make a roux with the shortening and flour. After roux is made, return meat to the pot with salt and pepper and tomato sauce. Simmer about 1 hour or until desired tenderness of meat is reached.

Mrs. O. P. Bordelon
Moreauville

Beef and Noodle Goulash

2 medium onions, chopped
2 bell peppers, chopped
3 or 4 tablespoons cooking oil or margarine
2 lbs. ground beef
1 tablespoon chili powder
¼ teaspoon garlic powder
Salt and pepper to taste
2 cups uncooked elbow macaroni
1 — 16 oz. can cream style corn
1 — 15 oz. can stewed tomatoes (blend in blender)
1 cup catsup
¾ lb. sharp cheddar cheese, grated

Saute onions and bell pepper in cooking oil or margarine until wilted. Add ground meat to onions and bell pepper. Cook until meat is brown. Add chili powder, salt and pepper. Boil elbow macaroni according to package directions, drain. Mix together meat mixture, cooked macaroni, corn, tomatoes, catsup and cheese. Put in large flat greased casserole dish. Bake uncovered in 350° oven for 45 minutes.

Makes 6-8 servings.

Carolyn B. Aymond
Lake Charles

No Peek Casserole

2 lbs. stew meat
2 tablespoons A-1 steak sauce
1 package onion soup mix
⅔ soup can water
1 can mushroom soup
1 — 2½ oz. can sliced mushrooms

Cut stew meat into bite-size pieces and put in large roasting pan with lid. Add other ingredients and mix well. Cook covered in 300° oven for 3 hours. DON'T PEEK. Serve over hot noodles with sour cream accompaniment.

NOTE: You can substitute wine for half of water.

Makes 8 servings.

Avona Stevenson
Jonesboro

Irish Stew

Chunks of cured bacon (not slices) raw
Chunks of steak meat, raw
Chunks of mutton, raw
Chunks of potatoes
Chunks of onions
Flour seasoned with pepper and salt
Iron Teflon pot with cover
Cold or warm water (approximately one cup)

Grease the pot. Line one layer of ingredients on top of the other as given above. After every layer of seasoned flour begin the procedure gain, until your pot has the amount you consider enough for the group. Then pour water over the last layer of seasoned flour, distributing it all the way around the top layer. Cover pot and place it over a low heat for 2 hours. Increase heat and allow to cook slowly for approximately 3 hours, or more, adjusting the heat according to need. Add other vegetables, carrots, parsnips, etc. if you desire.

Sister M. Theresine Cahill
Shreveport

Pork and Oyster Pie

⅓ cup oil
⅓ cup flour
1 cup chopped onion
¼ cup chopped green onion
1⅔ cup hot water
⅓ cup oysters.
1 lb. ground pork
¼ teaspoon salt
¼ teaspoon black pepper
Cayenne pepper to taste
Double pie crust
Beaten egg

Brown pork. Drain and set aside. Heat oil. Add flour, cook to dark brown stage. Add onions and continue cooking 8 minutes. Add green onions, hot water and oysters (with liquid), and pork, salt and pepper. Cook 15-20 minutes until very thick. Cool and make a double crust pie shell. Place mixture into shell. Brush top of crust with beaten egg (optional). Bake at 375° for 35-40 minutes or until brown.

Makes 6-8 servings.

Bee Troxler
Hahnville

Squirrel Sauce Piquante

3 squirrels
1 cup chopped celery
1 can tomato paste
1 cup chopped onion
1 cup chopped bell pepper
Salt and pepper to taste

Cut squirrels into serving pieces. Brown squirrel in large, heavy pot. Add seasonings and brown. Add tomato paste, salt and pepper and enough water to cover squirrel. Bring to boil and simmer until squirrel is tender. Serve over rice.

Makes 6-8 servings.

Mrs. Milton C. Daigre
Alexandria

Alligator Sauce Piquante

6 lb. alligator roast
1 cup cooking oil
1½ cups flour
1 medium onion, chopped
1 bell pepper, chopped
1 clove garlic, chopped
½ stalk celery, chopped
2 small cans tomato paste
Salt, black pepper, red pepper
Cooked rice

Season roast with salt and pepper. Make the roux: heat oil in iron skillet. When hot add flour, stirring constantly until well mixed. Lower heat and continue stirring until light brown. Add chopped onions, bell pepper, garlic and celery to roux and cook until wilted. Fill an oval roaster to the ¼ mark with water and begin heating. Add small amounts of roux-vegetable mixture to hot water, let dissolve, and add more until desired thickness. Add tomato paste and stir well. When dissolved, add alligator roast. Cover and cook at medium heat on top of stove for about 4 hours. When roast is done, remove center bone if desired. You may break meat into large chunks or small pieces. Serve over rice.

NOTE: Chicken, peeled shrimp or a pork roast may be substituted for the alligator.

Dee Mastalez
Jonesboro

Catfish filets a'la Normande

1 or 2 filets per person
3 or 4 tablespoons flour
½ stick oleo
Salt
Pepper
Juice of ½ lemon
Parsley flakes
¼ pint whipping cream

Dry fish filets in paper towels, dust each filet with flour. In a large frying pan, melt oleo over medium-high heat and fry filets about 5 minutes on each side. Salt and pepper to taste. Place each of filets on serving dish. Deglaze frying pan with lemon juice, then pour over filets. Add cream and sprinkle with parsley flakes. Bake in oven about 15 minutes. Serve with French fries or steamed potatoes.

Makes 4 servings.

Suzanne Grove
Coushatta

Crab Meat Au Gratin

1 stalk celery, chopped fine
1 cup onion, chopped fine
¼ lb. oleo or butter
½ cup flour
1 can evaporated milk (13 ozs.)
2 egg yolks
1 teaspoon salt
½ teaspoon red pepper
½ teaspoon black pepper
1 lb. crab meat
½ lb. grated cheddar cheese

Saute onions and celery in oleo until onions are wilted. Blend flour in with this mixture. Pour in milk gradually, stirring constantly. Add egg yolks, salt, red and black pepper; cook 5 minutes. Put crabmeat in bowl and pour cooked sauce over crabmeat. Blend well and put all in lightly greased casserole and sprinkle with cheese. Bake at 375° for 10-15 minutes.

Mrs. R. A. Bennett, Jr.
DeRidder

Crab Casserole

1 rib celery, chopped
2 large onions, chopped
4 cloves garlic, chopped
2 tablespoons cooking oil
3 eggs, well beaten
5 slices toasted white bread
1 small can evaporated milk
¼ can water
1 quart crabmeat
Salt and pepper to taste
1 tablespoon melted margarine

Cook celery, onions and garlic until wilted in oil. Combine beaten eggs, milk and water and soak bread, reserving ½ cup crumbs for topping. Combine wilted vegetables, soaked bread mixture and crabmeat. Season to taste. Pour into greased casserole; top with bread crumbs, and drizzle melted margarine over all. Bake in a 375° oven about ½ hour or until bread crumbs start to brown.

Mrs. Corrine M. Canik
Grand Chenier

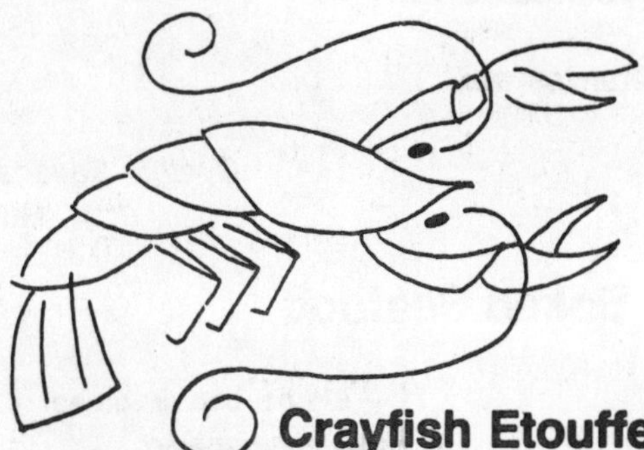

Crayfish Etouffee

5 lbs. crayfish tails, cleaned
½ lb. oleo
1¼ cup celery
2½ cups chopped onion
1¼ cup bell pepper
5 cloves garlic
5 cups water
½ cup parsley and onion tops
5 tablespoons cornstarch

Season tails well (salt and pepper), and set aside. Cook onion, garlic, celery and pepper in oleo. Add tails and ¾ cup of the water. Cook for 30 minutes, stirring occasionally. Dissolve cornstarch in remaining water and add to mixture with onion tops and parsley. Cook for 10 minutes more. Serve with rice.

Makes 8 servings.

Doris D. Ledoux
DeRidder

Shrimp Etouffee

1 stick butter or oleo
1 large onion, chopped
2 stalks celery, chopped
1 clove garlic, chopped
1 bunch green onions, chopped
Dash cayenne red pepper
Salt and pepper to taste
2 tablespoons cornstarch, mixed with 1 cup water
2 tablespoons tomato paste
2 lbs. shrimp, peeled and deveined

Melt butter in dutch oven on top of the stove. Add vegetables and saute just until tender; about 25 minutes. Add cornstarch and water stirring to blend. Stir in tomato paste. Add shrimp and turn fire to low. Simmer until shrimp begins to turn pink. Do not overcook. Add seasonings to taste, remove from heat. Serve over hot rice, with French bread and a green salad.

NOTE: The etouffee freezes well.

Cynthia Kavanaugh
Ruston

Baked Seafood

2 cups cooked rice
1 cup chopped celery
½ cup chopped green pepper
½ cup finely chopped onion
1 — 4½ oz. can water chestnuts, drained and sliced
2 — 4½ oz. cans of shrimp (may use fresh)
1 — 6½ oz. can crabmeat
1 cup mayonnaise
1 cup Snappy Tom tomato juice
¼ teaspoon salt
⅛ teaspoon pepper

Combine all ingredients, mix well and pour into 2½ quart casserole. Toast ½ cup sliced almonds in 1 tablespoon butter. Sprinkle casserole with nuts and 1 cup shredded cheddar cheese and paprika. Bake at 350° for 25 minutes.

Makes 8 servings.

Mrs. Robert (Charlotte) Morrison
Alexandria

Asparagus Casserole

1 large can asparagus tips
¼ lb. cracker crumbs
1 stick butter, melted
4 hard-boiled eggs, sliced
½ lb. grated cheese
½ cup almonds, sliced
1 cup mushroom soup

Grate cheese and mix well with cracker crumbs. Add liquid from asparagus to mushroom soup. Put layer of cracker crumbs and cheese mixture in bottom of casserole; add layer of asparagus; layer of eggs; layer of almonds; cover with mushroom soup. Repeat until all ingredients are used. Pour melted butter between each layer. End with layer of cheese and cracker crumbs and melted butter. Bake at 350° for 20 minutes.

Marjorie Thornton
Winnfield

Asparagus Pudding

3 slices bread, buttered and cut in small squares
1 can cut green asparagus (fresh can be used also)
1 cup diced cheddar cheese
3 beaten eggs
1 cup milk
Salt to taste

Use 1-quart casserole dish. Place or layer first 3 ingredients in dish in 2 layers of each ingredient. Cover with 1 cup of milk, to which has been added 3 beaten eggs and salt. Bake in 350° oven until eggs and milk are of custard consistency, approximately 40 minutes.

NOTE: Asparagus preferred by most without other vegetables.

Makes 4-6 servings.

Mrs. Don Crawford
Baton Rouge

Asparagus Souffle with Shrimp Almond Sauce

Asparagus Souffle:

1 — 10½ oz. can cream of mushroom soup
1 cup shredded sharp cheddar cheese
1 teaspoon nutmeg
½ cup chopped cooked asparagus
6 eggs, separated

Shrimp Almond Sauce:

1 — 10½ oz. can frozen cream of shrimp soup
⅓ cup water
2 tablespoons chopped almonds
1 tablespoon sherry

Makes 1½ cups sauce

Combine soup, cheese and nutmeg in saucepan; heat slowly until cheese is melted. Add asparagus. Beat egg yolks until thick and stir into soup mixture. Beat whites until stiff. Fold soup mixture into egg whites. Turn into a 2-quart casserole. Bake at 300° for 1-1¼ hours or until golden brown. Serve with sauce: combine all sauce ingredients listed. Heat, stirring occasionally.

Makes 4-6 servings.

Genevieve Kelley

Bean Casserole

1 — No. 2 can French sliced string beans
1 can cream of mushroom soup
1 can water chestnuts, sliced
1 can French fried onions
Salt to taste
Black pepper to taste
Worcestershire sauce to taste
1 tablespoon milk

Make mixture of soup, water chestnuts, milk and seasonings, with a little Worcestershire sauce. In a casserole dish (1-quart, greased) have first, a layer of onions, a layer of beans (drained), then a layer of the soup mixture. Season lightly with salt and pepper. Do this again for a second complete layer, then top it with a layer of the onions. Bake at 300° for 30-45-60 minutes (as you wish).

Makes 4 servings.

NOTE: Yellow rice and ham loaf go well with this, also broiled chicken.

Robert C. Ewig
Shreveport

Broccoli-Egg Casserole

3 or 4 slices bacon
1—10 oz. package frozen chopped broccoli or 2 cups chopped fresh broccoli
½ cup chopped onion
1 tablespoon butter or margarine
1 — 10¾ oz. can cream of mushroom soup, undiluted
½ teaspoon dry mustard
½ teaspoon salt
4 boiled eggs, chopped
1 cup shredded cheddar cheese

Fry bacon until crisp. Set aside and drain off grease. Cook broccoli in small amount of boiling water just until tender; drain and set aside. Saute onion in butter until tender; stir in soup, mustard and salt. Heat until bubbly. Arrange half of broccoli in a 1-quart casserole, top with half of chopped egg, half of cheese, and half of mushroom sauce. Repeat layers. Crumble bacon on top of casserole. Bake at 350° for 20-25 minutes. Yield: 6 servings.

Makes 6 servings.

Mrs. Wyly Gilfoil
Lake Providence

Brussels Sprouts and Chestnuts

3 — 10 oz. packages frozen brussels sprouts
2 tablespoons butter
2 teaspoons flour
¾ cup broth (chicken or beef)
Salt to taste
Pepper to taste
1½ cups sliced canned water chestnuts

Cook brussels sprouts according to directions on package. Make a sauce in double boiler with flour and broth and butter. Add sauce to brussels sprouts and chestnuts.

Makes 8 servings.

Mrs. Emily LaHaye
Ville Platte

Green Chili Casserole

6 cups boiling water
2 teaspoons salt
1 lb. Velveeta cheese
1 can diced green chilies
1 stick oleo
1½ cups grits
3 eggs, slightly beaten

Bring water to boil, add grits and cook slowly until thick. Add cheese (cut in pieces), green chilies and oleo, stirring until cheese melts. Beat in eggs. Pour into buttered casserole and cook 1 hour in 275° oven.

Mrs. Velda Barton
Winnfield

Cabbage Casserole

1 lb. Dizzy Dean sausage (or any other brand)
1 lb. ground meat
1 large bell pepper, chopped
1 head cabbage, chopped
2 onions, chopped
1 stick celery, chopped
1 can Rotel tomatoes, chopped
1 cup raw rice

Sauce:
1 lb. Velveeta cheese
1 lb. cheddar cheese
1 cup milk

Smother sausage, ground meat, pepper, onions and celery until browned. Then add cabbage and Rotel tomatoes and cook for about 10 minutes. Add the rice. Melt all of the sauce ingredients in a saucepan and pour it over the casserole in a dutch oven. Bake in a 350° oven for about 1½ hours.

Mrs. Eddie Simoneaux
Convent

Cabbage Rolls

1 large cabbage, cored
2½ teaspoons salt
4 quarts boiling water
1 onion, chopped
¼ cup butter
1½ cups cooked rice
1½ lbs. ground beef
¼ teaspoon white pepper
⅛ teaspoon allspice
¼ cup cold water

Cook whole cabbage 8 minutes in salted boiling water. Remove, cool slightly and separate leaves. Shred small center of cabbage left over. Saute shredded cabbage and onion in butter until tender. Mix onion and cabbage mixture into meat, rice and spice mixture. Mix well. Arrange mixture on individual cabbage leaves, fold leaves and secure with toothpicks. Cover, sprinkle water on rolls, and bake at 325° for 1 hour.

Sandra L. Theall
Abbeville

Stuffed Cabbage

2 cups cracked wheat — cook 20 minutes, salt to taste, cook as grits.

1 lb. ground beef, cook until gray in color, drain, salt and pepper to taste. Mix wheat and ground beef. Set aside (Cracked wheat can be obtained at health food stores.)

1 medium sized cabbage, quartered and cored. Cook about 4 or 5 minutes, drain and chop. Set aside.

1 stick margarine
2 medium onions, chopped
4 or 5 toes garlic, chopped
1 tablespoon celery seed
1 tablespoon parsley

Cook seasonings in margarine until onions are soft and clear. Set aside.

1 lb. Longhorn mild cheddar cheese, grated
¾ cup canned milk
½-¾ cups water
¾ cup seasoned bread crumbs

Mix cheese, milk, water and bread crumbs. In large casserole, place a layer each of chopped cabbage, ground meat and wheat, seasoning mixture, cheese and bread crumbs. Repeat layers ending with cheese and bread crumbs on top. Cover with aluminum foil and bake in 350° oven for 30-40 minutes until hot throughout.

NOTE: This makes a very large casserole. Hope you have an opportunity to try this recipe.

Mrs. Olga Ferrell
Chalmette

Corn Fritters

1 — 16 oz. can cream style corn
4 whole eggs
3 tablespoons salad oil
1 tablespoon sugar
1½ or 2 cups plain flour
1 teaspoon salt
3 teaspoons baking powder

Mix all ingredients together as listed, just enough to blend well. Heat deep fat, and drop the batter by spoonfuls into the deep fat. Let fry just to a golden brown and lift out onto paper towel or brown paper bag.

Makes about 50 fritters.

NOTE: These may be frozen and reheated in the oven. They are very good to accompany any meat dish or are very good served on pineapple or apple rings sauteed in oleo or butter. This recipe is easy to divide in half, using a small can of cream style corn. Good Luck!

Mrs. F. A. (Sadie) Babb
Lake Providence

Frankfurter Corn Bake

3 eggs, slightly beaten
2 — 17 oz. cans Del Monte cream style corn
1 cup fine dry bread crumbs
¼ cup finely chopped onions
1 teaspoon dry mustard
1 teaspoon salt
6-8 frankfurters, cut in ½" slices
Del Monte catsup (for garnish)

Beat eggs slightly in large bowl. Add remaining ingredients except catsup, saving out enough frankfurter slices to garnish top. Pour into well-greased shallow 1½ or 2-quart baking dish; arrange frankfurter garnish on top. Bake in moderately hot oven (375°) 30 minutes or until set in center. Garnish with catsup if desired.

Makes 6 servings.

Mrs. Harvey Dunn
Natalbany

Corn Pudding

2 — 16 oz. cans cream style corn
2 tablespoons sugar
½ cup flour
6 eggs
1 stick oleo
1 cup milk

In dish, 9¾×9¾×2", melt oleo; set aside. In large bowl mix corn, sugar and flour. Beat eggs, add to dry ingredients. Beat in milk and oleo. Pour into casserole dish and bake at 325° oven for 50 minutes or until knife inserted in center comes out clean.

Makes 8 servings.

Lila Mae Cupit
Delhi

Corn Pudding

1 — No. 303 can cream style corn
1 — No. 303 can whole kernel corn
1 large onion, chopped
1 medium bell pepper, chopped
1 — 2 oz. jar pimento, chopped
⅔ cup milk
1 egg, well-beaten
1 cup cracker crumbs
1 cup grated cheese
½ stick oleo, melted
2 tablespoons sugar
Salt and pepper to taste.

Combine all ingredients in order given; mix well. Pour into greased 2-quart baking dish. Bake for 1 hour in 350° oven.

Makes 8 servings.

Mrs. John T. Little
Monroe

Chinese Vegetables

1 package frozen green peas
1 can bean sprouts, drained
1 can water chestnuts, drained
1 large can mushrooms, drained and set aside
1 can cream of mushroom soup
½ cup American cheese
1 can French fried onions
Soy sauce to taste
Very little salt and pepper

Cook peas, drain and put in bottom of casserole dish which has been greased with butter. Add bean sprouts, water chestnuts (sliced thin), mushrooms. Dot with butter, season with salt and pepper and soy sauce. Spread mushroom soup on top and add a little juice from mushrooms. Grate cheese and sprinkle thickly on top. Cook 30 minutes in 350° oven. Take out and put warm French fried onions on top.

Mrs. W. T. Holloway
Jonesboro

Eggplant Casserole

1 medium-large eggplant
1 medium onion
1 large egg
¾ lb. grated processed cheese
1 cup milk
¼ lb. soda crackers, crumbled
Salt and pepper to taste

Peel eggplant and cut into ½″ cubes. Peel onion and chop. Stew for 10 minutes in covered saucepan with only enough water to avoid cooking dry. Drain liquid. In buttered baking dish arrange layers of cracker crumbs and stewed eggplant and onion mixture. Combine egg, cheese, milk, salt and pepper in blender. Blend until smooth. Pour liquid over ingredients in baking dish. Fork liquid into layers thoroughly. Bake at 350° for 45 minutes - 1 hour.

NOTE: Can be stored in refrigerator up to 5 days. Freezes for larger period. Serves 6-8.

Mary Nell Talbert
Leesville

Eggplant Dressing

2 medium eggplants
½ lb. ground chuck
½ lb. ground pork
1 large onion, chopped
2 ribs celery, chopped
1 medium bell pepper, chopped
4 cloves garlic, minced
½ cup cooking oil
1½ cups cooked rice (optional)
Buttered bread crumbs
Salt and pepper to taste

Peel and cube eggplant. In large pot, add enough water to cover cubes. Bring to boil. Cover and reduce heat to medium and cook until tender-crisp. Drain in colander. In ¼ cup oil, brown next 2 ingredients until red color disappears. Add next 4 ingredients and drained eggplant. Stir well, cover and cook on low heat until meat and vegetables are done (add a little water if dry). Turn into ovenproof casserole, sprinkle with bread crumbs. Bake 20-25 minutes in 325° oven. May be frozen before baking.

Patricia Calhoun
Lake Charles

Eggplant Casserole

½ cup butter
½ cup chopped onions
½ cup chopped bell pepper
½ cup chopped celery
½ cup chopped green onions
4 pods garlic, minced
1 medium eggplant, peeled and sliced
1½ cups grated cheese
1 cup cracker crumbs
1½ cups milk
4 eggs, beaten
Salt to taste
Pepper to taste
1 lb. raw shrimp, peeled and deveined (optional)

Set aside 1 tablespoon of the butter to dot top of casserole before baking. Melt remaining butter in a large skillet. Add next 5 ingredients and saute until tender. Add eggplant and cook over a medium heat, covered, until eggplant is mushy. Reserve ½ cup cheese and ¼ cup crumbs for topping. Combine cheese, crumbs, milk, eggs, salt and pepper in large mixing bowl. Stir in the eggplant mixture. Mix well. Bake in a greased 9×13″ baking pan. Sprinkle top with reserved cheese and crumbs. Dot with reserved butter. Bake in preheated oven at 350° for 30 minutes. If shrimp are used, add them to the sauteed onion mixture when the eggplant is added. The shrimp change this accompanying dish to a main dish. Makes 8-10 servings.

Carol Nunez
Bell City

Spanish Eggplant

2 cups cubed eggplant
½ cup chopped onion
½ cup chopped celery
¼ cup chopped green pepper
¼ cup butter or oleo
½ teaspoon salt
1 cup cubed fresh tomatoes

Soak eggplant in salted water for 10 minutes. Saute onion, celery and green pepper in butter or oleo. Add salt, tomatoes and drained eggplant. Cook covered for 20-25 minutes on medium heat. Serve as is or put in casserole. Heat when ready to serve.

NOTE: It is also good frozen. You may add sauteed ground beef for a main dish. Also crumbs and grated cheese are a good addition for variety.

Makes 6 servings.

Mrs. Joe D. Burns
Jonesboro

Eggplant and Shrimp

2 large eggplants
1 can cream of mushroom soup (undiluted)
1 medium onion, chopped fine
1 medium bell pepper, chopped
1 cup grated cheese (cheddar)
2 eggs, beaten
1 cup Ritz cracker crumbs (save few for topping)
1 can medium shrimp
Salt and pepper to taste

Peel, chop, and cook eggplant in salted water till tender and drain. Mix all other ingredients and pour in greased casserole dish. Cover with cracker crumbs, dot with butter and bake at 350° till bubbly and brown.

Makes 8-10 servings.

Celeste Edwards
Leesville

Seafood Stuffed Eggplant

1 large eggplant
1½ cups bread crumbs
¼ teaspoon black pepper
½ teaspoon salt
¼ cup snipped parsley
¼ cup chopped onions
¼ cup chopped celery
¼ cup chopped bell peppers
1 small can shrimp
1 small can crabmeat
1 small can oysters
¼ cup butter
1 egg, beaten

Cut eggplant in half, lengthwise. Cook covered in ½" boiling salt water for 10 minutes. Scoop out insides, saute onions, parsley, bell peppers and celery in butter. Combine eggplant pulp, crumbs, seasoning, seafood and eggs; if too dry add a little of the seafood juice. Mix well and refill eggplant shells. Sprinkle with extra bread crumbs and bake in 375° oven for 30 minutes.

Makes 4 servings.

A friend from Avoyelles Parish

Shrimp Eggplant Casserole

2 medium eggplants
1 large onion, chopped
½ cup celery, chopped
2 cloves garlic, minced
1 lb. shrimp
2 tablespoons butter or margarine, melted
4-6 slices day-old bread
1 cup water
½ cup chopped parsley
½ cup chopped onion tops
2 eggs, beaten
Salt to taste
Black and red pepper to taste
Progresso bread crumbs

Cook eggplants in boiling water about 15 minutes or until tender. Remove from water and let cool. Cut each in half, lengthwise. Carefully scoop out pulp. Chop pulp. Saute onions, celery and shrimp in butter until onion is clear and shrimp is tender. Soak bread in water, squeeze out any excess water. Add bread, parsley, onion tops, eggplant pulp, salt, black and red pepper to shrimp mixture. Cool slightly, then add beaten eggs, stirring well. Turn into a 1½-quart or 2-quart casserole. Top with Progresso bread crumbs. Bake at 350° uncovered for 35 minutes.

Hazel G. Deshotels
Ville Platte

Paulson's Louisiana "Hot Greens"

Greens
Pepper, few pods
½ cup vinegar
1 onion
Salt pork
Water

"The food you cook can be like the words of a song."

Wash enough greens to fill a pot,
A few pods of pepper to make them hot,
A half cup of vinegar, an onion, too,
Salt pork and water make a wonderful brew.
Boil them done on a medium heat,
"Why, hush yo' mouth, they're ready to eat."

Joseph B. Paulson
Shreveport

Shrimp Stuffed Mirliton

4 medium sized mirlitons
Seasoning (onion, garlic, celery, bell pepper)
1 lb. shrimp, finely chopped or coarsely ground
2 cups crumbled day-old bread
Salt and pepper to taste
½ can mushroom soup

Select well-shaped mirlitons, halve and core; boil in salted water for a few minutes until tender. Scoop out center of mirlitons, being careful not to cut through the peelings. Mash the mirliton pulp, mix with shrimp, crumbled bread crumbs (can be toasted) and desired amount of minced seasoning. Stuff each half, sprinkle with Italian seasoned bread crumbs and parmesan cheese, if desired. Carefully add mushroom soup around sides of baking dish. Bake in a medium oven until browned, about ½ hour.

Makes 8 servings.

Mrs. Reece Chenevert, Cottonport
Mrs. Winnie S. Thibodaux, Slidell

Cheesy Onion Casserole

5 medium onions, thinly sliced
¼ cup butter or margarine
¼ cup all-purpose flour
2 cups milk
2 cups (½ lb.) shredded sharp cheese
½ teaspoon salt
½ teaspoon pepper

Separate onion slices into rings, place in an ungreased 2½-quart casserole. Melt butter in a heavy saucepan over low heat, blend in flour, cook until bubbly, stirring constantly. Gradually add milk, cook over low heat until bubbly, stirring constantly about 6 minutes or until thickened. Stir in cheese, salt and pepper. Cook just until cheese melts. Remove sauce from heat, pour over onions mixing gently. Bake at 325° for 45-50 minutes.

Makes 6-8 servings.

Miss Lillian Hermann
Hammond

Early Peas Casserole

1 medium onion, sliced
½ bar butter
1 can mushroom soup
1 small can sliced mushrooms, drained
½ cup chopped almonds
4 hard-cooked eggs, sliced
1 cup water chestnuts
1 tablespoon Worcestershire sauce
Salt and pepper to taste
2 — 17 oz. cans Pride of Illinois peas, drained

Saute onions in butter until tender. Combine onion, butter, soup, mushrooms, almonds, water chestnuts, Worcestershire sauce, salt and pepper. Gently fold in peas. Place half of this mixture in a buttered 12×9×2″ casserole; top with sliced eggs. Add remaining pea mixture, top with the other 2 sliced eggs. Bake at 350° for 15 minutes.

Makes 8 servings.

Mrs. Marine H. Dupas
Moreauville

Yum Yum Stuffed Peppers

- 8 medium bell peppers
- 1 lb. ground meat
- ⅔ cup Italian bread crumbs
- ½ teaspoon salt
- ¼ teaspoon pepper
- ¼ cup chopped bell pepper
- ¼ cup chopped onions
- 2-3 toes chopped garlic
- 2 eggs
- ½ cup cold water
- ¼ cup bread crumbs

Clean and wash peppers. Save tops to chop into mix later. In a large 3-quart bowl, mix together well all of the next ingredients including chopped tops of peppers. Stuff into pepper shells. When all peppers are stuffed, dip tops of peppers into topping bread crumbs. Brown tops in a teflon skillet until bread crumbs are light brown. Place on a pot rack in a saucepan or medium skillet. Add ½ cup water to pot and cook uncovered until water is steaming, about 4-5 minutes. Then cover pot, leave slightly open for steam to escape and continue to cook for about 1 hour. Check to be sure there is still water in the pot about every 12-15 minutes and if necessary add ⅓ to ½ cup water when needed. Serve in shells. Preparation and cooking time is about 1 hour and 30 minutes.

Norma D. Theriot
Slidell

Unstuffed Peppers

- 1 lb. ground beef (extra lean beef)
- 1 cup chopped onions
- 2 medium sized green peppers, cut in strips
- 1 teaspoon salt
- ¼ teaspoon ground pepper
- 2 cups cooked rice
- ½ cup catsup

In a large skillet, cook ground beef over moderately high heat, breaking it up with a spoon, until fat starts to cook out and meat has just begun to brown. Stir in onions, green peppers, salt and pepper. Cook about 3 minutes longer, stirring once or twice, until meat is all light brown. Spoon off and discard as much fat as possible. Stir in cooked rice and just enough catsup to hold the mixture together. Cover skillet; reduce heat to moderately low and cook 8-10 minutes longer, until rice is hot and peppers are tender. Makes about 6 cups or 4-6 servings.

NOTE: Good with carrot and zucchini strips, with a yogurt and lemon sherbet for dessert. Per one-sixth of recipe: 297 calories, 16 grams protein, 16 grams fat, 21 grams carbohydrate.

Leigh Wimberly
Leesville

Baked Stuffed White Potatoes

4 large white baking potatoes
4 tablespoons sour cream
¼ cup heavy cream
3 tablespoons butter
Snipped parsley for garnish
Salt, pepper, and paprika to taste
5 tablespoons chopped green onions (tops and bottoms)
6 slices bacon (fried and crumbled)
2 tablespoons grated parmesan cheese

Wash and dry potatoes. Bake potatoes for 1 hour and 10 minutes or until cooked. Saute onions in butter until wilted, fry bacon and crumble. After potatoes are cooked, remove part of top, scrape potato from shell and mash until creamed; add sour cream, onions, bacon, cheese, salt, pepper and paprika. Return mixture to shell and sprinkle with bacon. Place in oven at 375° for 20 or 25 minutes until potatoes are well heated.

Makes 4 servings.

Mrs. Marine H. Dupas
Moreauville

Potato-Broccoli Casserole

2 tablespoons butter
2 tablespoons all-purpose flour
1 teaspoon salt
⅛ teaspoon pepper
2 cups milk
⅛ teaspoon nutmeg, freshly
1 — 3 oz. package cream cheese
½ cup shredded Swiss cheese
4 cups—16 oz. package hash brown potatoes, thawed
1 — 10 oz. package frozen chopped broccoli, cooked and drained
¼ cup fine bread crumbs
1 tablespoon butter

Make a white sauce by melting 2 tablespoons butter, blend in flour and season with salt, pepper and nutmeg. Add milk gradually. Cook and stir until bubbly. Add cubed cream cheese and Swiss cheese and stir until melted. Stir in hash browns. Turn half the mixture into a 10×6×2″ baking dish and top with broccoli. Spoon remaining cheese sauce mixture over broccoli. (Can be frozen at this point.) Bake covered in 350° oven 35 minutes. Mix crumbs and remaining butter and sprinkle around edges and bake uncovered 10-15 minutes.

Mrs. Lloyd Manuel
Kinder

Potato Casserole

2 lbs. frozen hash brown potatoes
½ cup melted butter or margarine
½ teaspoon salt
½ teaspoon black pepper
1 — 8 oz. can cream of chicken soup
2 — 4 oz. cartons sour cream
2 teaspoons onion flakes
10 ozs. grated cheddar cheese

Thaw potatoes. Combine all ingredients and place in greased casserole dish. Bake 1 hour at 350°. During last 15 minutes top with crushed Ritz crackers or corn flakes or bread crumbs.

Sandra B. Edmonson, Greenwell Springs
Dula Mae Roby, Jonesboro

Potatoes Gourmet

6 medium potatoes
2 cups shredded cheddar cheese
6 tablespoons butter, divided
1½ cups commercial sour cream
3 green onions, chopped
1 teaspoon salt
¼ teaspoon white pepper

Cook potatoes in skins, cool. Peel and shred on a coarse grater or in the food processor. Combine cheese and 4 tablespoons butter in saucepan; heat and stir until cheese is almost melted. Remove from heat and blend in sour cream, onions, salt and pepper. Fold in potatoes and spoon into a greased 2-quart casserole. Dot with 2 tablespoons butter. Cover and bake at 300° about 25 minutes or until hot.

NOTE: This recipe can be frozen before baking.

Mrs. Lloyd Manuel
Kinder

Sweet Potato Casserole

3 cups cooked, mashed sweet potatoes
1 cup sugar
2 eggs
⅓ cup Carnation milk
½ cup butter
1 cup firmly packed brown sugar
⅓ cup all-purpose flour
⅓ cup butter
2 cups finely chopped pecans

Combine sweet potatoes, sugar, eggs, vanilla, milk and ½ cup butter; beat with electric mixer until smooth. Spoon into a greased 2-quart shallow casserole. Combine brown sugar, flour, ⅓ cup butter and pecans, sprinkle over top of casserole. Bake at 350° for 30 minutes.

Makes 10 servings.

Mrs. Marine H. Dupas
Moreauville

Squash Casserole

1 onion, chopped
1 bell pepper, chopped
3 cups cooked squash,
(salt, pepper, sugar to taste
1 stick margarine
2 eggs, beaten
2 cups grated cheese
1 cup cream of mushroom soup
1 cup bread crumbs

In margarine, saute onions and pepper until tender, add squash and eggs. Add grated cheese (reserve half cup for top); sprinkle bread crumbs on top; add mushroom soup on top and sprinkle with cheese. Bake about 35 minutes at 350°.

Jewel Tison
Colfax

Squash Casserole

4 cups cooked yellow summer squash
1 teaspoon salt
½ teaspoon pepper
1 carrot, grated
1 stick oleo, melted
1 carton sour cream
1 can cream of chicken soup
3 cups Pepperidge Farm crumbs (or bread crumbs plus 1 teaspoon sage)

Blend together first 6 ingredients. Melt oleo in saucepan, add crumbs and toss together. Pour half of the crumb mixture into bottom of baking dish (13×9×2"). Pour squash mixture over top of crumbs; add remaining crumbs on top. Bake 30 minutes in 350° oven.

Makes 8 servings.

Mrs. John T. Little
Monroe

Golden Cheese Squash

2 lbs. yellow summer squash
2 slightly beaten egg yolks
1 cup sour cream
2 tablespoons all-purpose flour
2 stiffly beaten egg whites
1½ cups grated cheddar cheese
6 slices bacon (crisp cooked, drained, and crumbled)
½ cup bread crumbs
1 tablespoon butter, melted

Clean squash and trim off ends. Do not peel. Cut in ¼″ slices and sprinkle lightly with salt. Cook in steamer rack for 15 minutes. (You should have about 6 cups.) Reserve a few slices for garnish. Stir together egg yolks, sour cream and flour. Fold in the stiffly beaten egg whites. In a 12×7×2″ pyrex dish layer half the squash, then half the egg mixture, and half the grated cheese and half bacon crumbs. Repeat layer. Combine bread crumbs with melted butter and place on top around edges, arrange garnish slices down the middle. Bake 20-25 minutes in 350° oven.

Makes 6-8 servings.

Mrs. W. J. (Mae) Trahan, Jr.
Bossier City

Ritz Squash Casserole

4 cups cooked and drained yellow squash
1 cup mild grated cheese
1 can cream of mushroom soup
1 onion, finely chopped
2 beaten eggs
Salt and pepper to taste
1 cup coarse Ritz Cracker crumbs (about 20 crackers)
Reserve some crumbs to sprinkle on top

Mix in order given and bake at 350° until it bubbles.

Makes 8 servings.

Leaoto Martin
Shreveport

Squash Delight

1 lb. yellow squash
1 stick oleo or butter
½ cup chopped onion
½ cup chopped bell pepper
½ cup grated cheddar cheese
Red pepper to taste
½ cup sliced water chestnuts
½ cup mayonnaise (Hellmans recommended)
1 teaspoon sugar
1 egg, beaten

Slice and cook squash until tender. Drain squash, add other ingredients, mix well. Place in casserole, cover with bread crumbs, dot with butter or oleo. Bake uncovered in 350° oven for 30-40 minutes.

NOTE: Squash can be increased to 1½ lbs. for less rich dish. This freezes very well.

Makes 10-12 servings.

Mrs. John W. Riley, Winnfield
Callie Jones, Coushatta

Sweet Tater Balls

4 sweet potatoes
¼ teaspoon cinnamon
¼ teaspoon ground cloves
½ stick margarine or butter
1 teaspoon vanilla
6 large marshmallows
Coconut or cornflakes

Wash and dry sweet potatoes and grease. Bake in 350° oven until done (about 1½ hours). Peel and mash; add seasonings. Cover large marshmallows with mixture. Roll in cornflakes or coconut. Bake in 325° oven until coconut is browned or until hot.

Makes 6 servings.

Mrs. J. P. Kelley
Alexandria

Farce de Potato Douce (Sweet Potato Dressing)

1 turkey neck and giblets
2 cups mashed sweet potatoes
1 cup mashed Irish potatoes
1 lb. country-seasoned pork sausage
1 lb. ground beef
1 cup chopped celery
1 cup chopped lettuce
1 cup chopped onions
½ cup chopped bell peppers
¼ cup chopped shallots
½ teaspoon black pepper
1 tablespoon Worcestershire sauce
1 sprig chopped parsley
1 teaspoon salt

Boil turkey neck and giblets until tender; boil broth down to about 1 cup. Remove from water, debone neck; chop finely with giblets. Set broth aside. Boil sweet potatoes and irish potatoes in jacket until tender. Peel and mash separately. Measure and set aside. In large deep skillet, saute sausage and ground beef. Add chopped turkey neck and giblets; cook about 5 minutes, stirring constantly. Add chopped celery, lettuce, onions, bell pepper, shallots and cook until soft on low fire. Add potatoes and all other ingredients and about ½ cup of the broth. Cover skillet tightly and cook over low heat approximately 1 hour, stirring occasionally to prevent sticking. Add broth as needed to prevent from sticking. Serve in casserole with turkey. Serves about 20 people.

Clara Englade
Reserve

Sweet Potato Souffle

3 cups cooked sweet potatoes
½ cup sugar
½ cup Pet milk
½ stick oleo
2 eggs, beaten well
1 teaspoon vanilla

Topping:
3 cups corn flakes, crushed
¾ cup brown sugar
½ teaspoon oleo
1 cup chopped nuts

Mix potatoes, sugar, milk, oleo, eggs & vanilla well. Pour into a well-greased casserole pan and bake at 350° for 25 minutes.

Topping: Mix corn flakes, sugar, oleo and nuts together by hand and put on top of sweet potatoes. Bake about 10 minutes.

Linda Giroir
New Orleans

Turnip Casserole

6 cups mashed turnips
1 stick oleo
Bread or cornflake crumbs
1¼ cups sugar
1 — 8 oz. package cream cheese

Boil and salt enough turnips to make six mashed cups. Add softened oleo, cream cheese and sugar. Pour into greased casserole dish and cover with bread crumbs. Bake at 350° for 30 minutes.

Makes 6-8 servings.

NOTE: Rutabagas or carrots may also be used in place of turnips.

Sis Walters
Leesville

Baked Zucchini Provolone

3 cups green zucchini squash,
1 onion, sliced or chopped
2 cups canned tomatoes in puree
1 cup water
2 tablespoons bread crumbs
Oregano or Italian seasoning
4 ozs. sharp provolone cheese, chopped
¼ teaspoon pepper
1 teaspoon garlic salt

Place ingredients in order listed, in layers, in greased baking dish. Bake at 350° for 25-30 minutes.

Makes 10 servings.

Kathryn Billeaud
Luling

Stuffed Zucchini

2 zucchini squash
½ cup oleo or butter
1 large onion, chopped fine
1 small bell pepper, chopped fine
2 ribs celery, chopped fine
1 clove garlic, chopped fine
1½ cups cleaned, deveined shrimp, chopped
½ lb. crabmeat
Salt and pepper to taste
1 cup bread crumbs
2 tablespoons parsley, chopped

Zucchini should be cut in half, lengthwise. Scoop center with grapefruit knife or paring knife. Melt butter or oleo and simmer vegetables — onions, bell pepper, celery, garlic and zucchini until tender. Add shrimp, crabmeat, bread crumbs and parsley to hot vegetables. Mix well with salt and pepper to taste. Stuff in zucchini shell. Bake in shallow pan for 30 minutes at 350°. Garnish with boiled shrimp. Shell may also be eaten.

Makes 4-8 servings.

Mrs. William (Rea) Gilbert
Thibodaux

Cheese Grits Casserole

1 cup Aunt Jemima quick grits
4 cups water
1 teaspoon salt
1 stick oleo
1 roll Kraft garlic cheese
½ roll Kraft Jalapeno cheese
2 eggs
½ cup milk

Bring 4 cups water to a boil, add salt and grits, cook 5 minutes. Remove from heat and add: 1 stick oleo, 1 roll garlic cheese, ½ roll Jalapeno cheese, 2 eggs well beaten with ½ cup milk. Return to stove and cook about five minutes stirring until oleo and cheese melt. Pour into buttered casserole and bake 30 minutes in 350° oven or until set. Sprinkle top with paprika if desired.

Makes 8-10 servings.

Eloise M. Harbin
Lake Providence

Green Rice

1 lb. bulk hot sausage (Bryan or Jimmy Dean)
1 cup chopped bell pepper
1 cup chopped green onion
½ cup parsley flakes (dried)
1 cup raw rice
2 — 8 oz. cans Campbells beef broth

Mix all ingredients together with fork and place in 2-quart casserole. Cover with foil and bake 1½ hours at 350°. (Check after one hour of cooking; you don't want this to be too dry.)

Makes 6 servings.

NOTE: May be made ahead of time and stored in refrigerator and cooked next day.

Clarice Madden
Ringgold

Green Rice

1 stick oleo or butter
1 onion, chopped
2 ribs celery, chopped
2 packages frozen broccoli
1 can cream of chicken soup
1 can cream of mushroom soup
1 small jar Cheese Whiz
1 — 6 oz. can mushrooms
1 cup chopped almonds
2 cups rice, cooked
Salt and pepper to taste
Bread crumbs
Butter

Saute onions and celery in butter until light yellow in color. Mix the partially cooked broccoli with both soups and cheese; add to celery and onions. Stir in the rice, mushrooms, almonds and seasonings. Pour into a large-greased casserole and top with buttered bread crumbs. Bake at 350° for 45 minutes.

Makes at least 12 servings.

NOTE: This makes a very large dish. If desired, place in two casserole dishes and freeze one (before baking) for use at a later time.

LaVerne Nalley
Quitman

Red Beans and Rice with Sausage

1 lb. red beans
½ lb. ham or salt pork
2 quarts water
3 cups chopped onion
1 bunch green onions, chopped
1 cup chopped parsley
1 cup chopped bell pepper
2 pods garlic, crushed
1 tablespoon salt
1 teaspoon red pepper
1 teaspoon black pepper
3 big dashes Tabasco sauce
3 links smoked sausage (about 1 lb.)
1 small 8 oz. can tomato sauce
¼ teaspoon oregano
¼ teaspoon thyme
1 tablespoon Worchestershire

Cook beans and ham in the water slowly for 45 minutes. Add all the vegetables, seasonings and tomato sauce to mixture. Cook slowly for 1 hour. Add more water if needed. Add sausage that has been cut in thin slices and cook 45 minutes more. Remove from the heat and cool. Reheat and bring to a boil, then simmer for 30-40 minutes. Serve this over hot white rice.

NOTE: The red pepper may be omitted for a milder taste or for children. Use a large pot to prepare as for gumbo.

Makes 16 servings.

Mrs. Lamonte (Carol) Massey
Jonesboro

Sausage Rice Casserole

1 lb. roll hot sausage
1 cup rice
1 bell pepper, chopped
1 onion, chopped
1 cup chopped celery
6 cups boiling water
2 packages Lipton chicken noodle soup

Brown sausage and drain off grease. Add chopped vegetables and rice. Bring water to boil and add soup mix. Boil 1 minute. Mix all together and bake 1 hour at 375°.

Makes 10 servings.

Birdie C. Honeycutt
Dry Prong

Rice and Seafood Supreme

½ cup chopped onions
⅔ cup chopped bell pepper
2 small cloves garlic
1 cup diced celery
4 sprigs parsley
¼ cup pimento
¼ cup margarine or butter
2 teaspoons salt
¼ teaspoon red pepper
1 teaspoon black pepper
1 — 10½ oz. can mushroom soup
1 can crabmeat
1½ cups shrimp
3 cups cooked rice

Saute onions, bell pepper, garlic, celery, parsley and pimento in the margarine. Add salt and pepper. Mix until blended. Add soup and stir well. Add crabmeat, shrimp and rice. Mix well without mashing grains. Pour into greased casserole dish. Bake 20 minutes in a moderate oven at 400°.

NOTE: You can top casserole with 1 cup bread crumbs, tossed with 2 tablespoons butter.

Arnie Murphy
Ringgold

Stir Fried Rice

½ cup cooked ham, diced
2 eggs
2 tablespoons green peas
2 tablespoons carrots
1 tablespoon chopped green onion
4 cups cooked rice
2 teaspoons salt
8 tablespoons corn oil

Heat 2 tablespoons of the oil in pan. Pour in beaten eggs and stir fry quickly until eggs are in tiny pieces. Remove from pan. Heat another 3 tablespoons of the oil. Stir fry diced ham, green peas and carrots about 1 minute and remove from pan. Heat the remaining 3 tablespoons oil in pan. Stir fry green onion and cooked rice; mix well. Add salt. Reduce heat and keep stirring until rice is thoroughly heated. Combine rice with egg, green peas and carrots and serve.

NOTE: Shrimp, chicken or roast pork may be substituted for cooked ham.

Makes 4 servings.

Tina Chou
Ruston

Baked Macaroni and Cheese

2 cups elbow macaroni (8 ozs.)
1 tablespoon salt
3 quarts boiling water
4 tablespoons butter
1 tablespoon flour
½ teaspoon salt
¼ teaspoon celery seed
⅛ teaspoon pepper
2 cups milk
1¼ lbs. process American cheese, grated
2 tablespoons seasoned bread crumbs

Gradually add macaroni and 1 tablespoon salt to rapidly boiling water. Cook uncovered, stirring occasionally until tender. Drain in colander, rinse under cold running water. Meanwhile, melt 2 tablespoons butter in saucepan, blend in flour, ½ teaspoon salt, celery salt and pepper. Stir in milk and cook; stir until thickens. Add cheese, stir until melted. Combine macaroni and cheese sauce and mix well. Melt remaining butter and toss lightly with bread crumbs. Place macaroni mixture in 1½-quart casserole and sprinkle crumbs on top. Bake at 400° for 15-20 minutes or until lightly browned and bubbly.

Makes 6 servings.

Mrs. Marine H. Dupas
Moreauville

Pork Tasso Cornbread Dressing

½ cup chopped onion
¾ cup chopped bell pepper
1 cup chopped celery
½ cup margarine
2 cups cornbread
4 sprigs parsley, chopped
1 whole pimento, chopped
1 can cream of mushroom soup
4 cloves garlic, chopped
2 cups tasso, cut up very small

Cook onions, bell pepper, celery, pimento, parsley, garlic and tasso in margarine until tender. Add crumbled cornbread and mix well. Stir in soup, then season to taste. Place in buttered casserole dish and bake 30 minutes at 400°.

Makes 4-6 servings.

NOTE: Tasso is strips of smoked pork.

Mrs. Donald A. Mayeux
Mamou

Italian Casserole

1 large onion, chopped
2 bunches green onions, chopped
2 lbs. ground beef
2 tablespoons flour
1 large can mushroom bits and pieces
24 ozs. tomato sauce
Salt and pepper to taste
8 ozs. cream cheese
8 ozs. cottage cheese
8 ozs. sour cream
1 small package vermicelli noodles
2 tablespoons oleo

Brown ground beef with onions. Add flour. Add drained mushrooms and tomato sauce. Salt and pepper to taste. In another bowl, mix cream cheese, cottage cheese and sour cream. Set aside. Cook vermicelli noodles, drain and mix with oleo. Use one large or several small casseroles. Put a layer of noodles, layer of cheese mixture, and layer of meat sauce. Bake at 375° for 30 minutes or till hot through.

Makes 10-12 servings.

Jane S. Bolton
Jonesboro

Spaghetti Sauce

1½ lbs. ground chuck
Salt to taste
Pepper to taste
2 medium onions, chopped
2 large bell peppers, chopped
1 package French's Italian Spaghetti sauce mix
4 — 8 oz. cans tomato sauce
(More spices can be added depending on taste)

Brown meat, onions and bell pepper, salt and pepper. Continue cooking until onions and bell pepper are tender. Pour in the sauce mix and stir, add tomato sauce and 2 cans of water. Stir and bring to boil. Cover and simmer about 2 hours under low heat.

Mrs. Theresa Lowery
Winnfield

You Are Too Sweet

Often it is easier to slip from gormet to gourmand in the dessert department. And a lot more fun too!

Something about our sweet tooth that holds out longer at the table and makes those desserts taste so-o good even when our good sense tells us no!

Our contributors here have tempted us in just such a fashion and we are going to have at them—no holds barred!!

Diabetic Cake

1¼ cups flour (plain)
2 teaspoons soda
1 teaspoon cinnamon
¼ teaspoon nutmeg
½ teaspoon salt
½ cup soft butter or margarine
1 teaspoon vanilla
1 egg
2 teaspoons powdered sweetener
2 cups freshly grated apple
½ cup chopped nuts

Mix first 5 ingredients, then add butter, vanilla, egg and powdered sweetener. Add grated apple and chopped nuts last. Pour into 8″ square greased and floured pan. Bake at 375° for 40-45 minutes.

Makes 12 servings.

Mrs. R. M. Reeves
Jena

Fig Cake

2 cups sugar
1 cup cooking oil
2 cups plain flour
1 teaspoon baking soda
1 teaspoon salt
1 cup milk
3 eggs
1 teaspoon cinnamon
½ teaspoon nutmeg
1 teaspoon vinegar
1 cup cooked figs
1 cup chopped pecans

Mix all ingredients in order of listing, stirring after each addition. Bake in a greased and floured 9×13″ pan at 300° for 30-45 minutes until done.

Makes 10-12 servings.

Hilda Keene
Jena

Ice Box Fruit Cake

1 lb. box graham crackers, crushed
1 stick butter or margarine
1 lb. marshmallows
1 small jar cherries, chopped
1 cup chopped pecans

Line graham cracker box with foil. Melt marshmallows in the butter. Mix cherries and pecans. Add marshmallow mixture and cherry-pecan mixture to graham cracker crumbs in a bowl. Pour into foil-lined box and keep in the refrigerator.

Beverly Dyson
Grand Chenier

Fudge Cake

1 stick butter
1 cup sugar
½ cup flour
2 tablespoons cocoa
2 eggs
½ cup pecans, chopped
1 teaspoon vanilla

Preheat oven to 350°. Line 8″ square pan with wax paper, bottom and sides. Melt butter, add sugar, flour and cocoa. Mix well, then add 2 eggs. Beat until well blended. Add vanilla and pecans. Pour into pan and bake 30 minutes. Remove from pan and remove wax paper immediately. It is easier to cut while hot. Cut into small squares.

NOTE: This will keep moist in a well-covered container for a week.

Mrs. Reynolds Bath
Alexandria

Gingerbread Upside-Down Apple Cake

¼ cup butter
½ cup brown sugar (packed)
2 cups peeled, thinly sliced apples
Small bottle cherries
½ cup pecan halves
1 box gingerbread mix

Heat oven to 350°. Melt ¼ cup butter in 9″ square pan. Blend in ½ cup brown sugar. Spread mixture over bottom of pan. Over this, overlap 3 rows of peeled, thinly sliced apples. Between rows of apple slices, alternate cherry halves and pecan halves. Make gingerbread as directed on package. Pour into prepared pan. Bake 35-40 minutes. Immediately place a plate over pan and turn pan the plate upside down. Allow sugar mixture to run down over cake. Remove pan. Cut in squares.

NOTE: Serve warm with whipped cream or ice cream.

Makes 9 servings.

Mrs. Elsie Watts
Winnfield

Martha Washington Cake with Whiskey Icing

1 cup shortening
2 cups sugar
4 egg yolks
1 teaspoon vanilla
3 cups flour, pre-sifted
¼ teaspoon salt
3 teaspoons baking powder
1 cup milk
4 egg whites, stiff-beaten

Whiskey Icing:

¼ lb. butter (no substitute)
Pinch salt
Powdered sugar
Whiskey

Thoroughly cream shortening and sugar. Add egg yolks and vanilla; beat well. Add sifted dry ingredients alternately with milk. Fold in stiff-beaten egg whites. Pour batter into greased and floured angel food cake pan. Bake in preheated 350° oven for 50-55 minutes or until surface springs back when gently pressed with fingertip. Cool in pan 10 minutes. Remove and cool thoroughly on wire rack.

Whiskey Icing: Moisten with good whiskey. Beat until creamy and of correct consistency to spread on cake top and about halfway down the side of cake.

Mrs. W. B. (Melba) Ragland, Jr.
Lake Providence

Mississippi Mud Cake

4 eggs
2 cups sugar
2 sticks melted margarine
1½ cups sifted flour
⅓ cup cocoa
1 teaspoon vanilla
1 cup coconut
1-2 cups pecans
1 — 7 oz. jar marshmallow cream

Frosting:

1 stick melted margarine
6 tablespoons milk
⅓ cup cocoa
1 box powdered sugar
1 teaspoon vanilla
1-2 cups nuts

Beat eggs and sugar until thick. Combine oleo, flour, cocoa, vanilla, coconut and nuts. Mix well and add to sugar mixture. Pour into greased and floured 9×13″ pan and bake 30 minutes at 350°. Immediately after removing from oven spread jar of marshmallow cream over top. Let set 30 minutes. While cake is still warm, frost it.

Frosting: Melt oleo, remove from heat. Add all other ingredients except nuts. Beat well and spread gently over marshmallow cream. When cake is cool, cut into squares.

Agnes Meeken, Colfax
Phyllis L. Dartez, Abbeville

Butter Pound Cake

3 cups of sugar
1 stick of butter (room temperature)
6 eggs
3 cups of Soft & Silk flour or Swan flour
1 small carton of whip cream
2 teaspoons vanilla extract

Mix all ingredients and let stand for 20 minutes. Place in oven at 300°-325° for 3 hours or until done.

Makes 12 servings.

Ms. Stella L. Bradix Thomas
Algiers

Black Walnut Cake

Cake:

½ cup shortening
½ cup margarine
2 cups sugar
5 eggs, separated
2 cups sifted flour
1 teaspoon baking soda
1 cup buttermilk
1 package black walnuts

Cream first 3 ingredients until fluffy. Add egg yolks one at a time, beating well after each. Sift flour and soda. Add alternately with buttermilk, beginning and ending with flour mixture. Beat egg whites until stiff, fold into batter. Add walnuts, saving some for top. Pour into 3 greased and floured pans. Bake at 350° for 25-30 minutes. Cool and frost.

Icing:

½ cup margarine
1 — 8 oz. package cream cheese, softened
1 lb. box powdered sugar
⅛ teaspoon vanilla
⅛ teaspoon salt

Mix all ingredients together and ice cake. Sprinkle remaining walnuts on top.

Jackie Burroughs
Shreveport

Cold Oven Pound Cake

3 cups plain flour
1½ teaspoons baking powder
3 cups sugar
½ lb. margarine
½ cup shortening
5 eggs
1 cup milk
2 teaspoons vanilla

Sift flour and baking powder together. Set aside. Cream margarine, shortening and sugar together. Add eggs, one at a time, to sugar mixture. Blend well after each addition. Add flour alternately with milk to sugar mixture. Add vanilla. Beat for 10 minutes. Pour into a well-greased and floured tube pan. Place in cold oven. Turn oven to 350° for 1 hour and 15 minutes.

Mrs. Joe Ann Brown
West Monroe

Christmas Dessert: Tipseys Squire

Sponge Cake (bake 2 weeks to 1 month early):

4 eggs
1¾ cups sugar
1 cup boiling water
2½ cups flour
4 teaspoons baking powder
1 teaspoon vanilla

Custard:

2 cups milk
3 eggs
Almonds, chopped
¼ cup sugar
⅛ teaspoon salt
Vanilla
Whipping Cream
Cherries

Sponge Cake: Separate eggs. Beat 1 egg white very stiff. Add 4 yolks and beat well. Gradually add sugar and boiling water, beat until smooth. Sift flour and baking powder, add to mixture, add vanilla. Fold in remaining egg whites, stiffly beaten. Bake 50-60 minutes at 350°. Cool, wrap in cheese cloth and store in dry place for 2 weeks to 1 month.

Custard: Scald milk, beat eggs slightly, add sugar and salt. Add milk slowly to egg mixture, return to double boiler and cook until spoon coats, stirring constantly. Add vanilla. The custard should not be made until after the sponge cake has dried out. After cake is dried and hard, cut in bite size strips, place in deep bowl. Cover with sliced almonds, build layers to top of bowl. Sprinkle with 2-4 tablespoons bourbon and let stand 24 hours, covered. Make the custard and pour over cake and let stand 12 hours. Whip cream cut half gently into cake until soft. Top cake with balance of whipped cream and cherries.

Makes 6-8 servings.

NOTE: Serve in compotes — it is delicious and colorful.

Mrs. David Wilson
Shreveport

Christmas Zucchini Bread

2 cups sugar
1 cup butter or oleo
3 eggs
2 cups grated zucchini
1 teaspoon vanilla
3 cups all-purpose flour
¼ teaspoon baking powder
1 teaspoon baking soda
½ teaspoon salt
1 teaspoon cinnamon
1 teaspoon cloves, ground
½ teaspoon allspice
¼ teaspoon nutmeg
¼ teaspoon ginger
1 cup raisins
1 cup chopped nuts
1 cup mixed crystallized fruit

Shred raw zucchini, omitting big seeds. Blend sugar and butter; add eggs, mix well. Stir in zucchini. Add vanilla. Combine flour, baking powder, baking soda, salt and spices and add to egg mixture. Reserve about ½ cup of flour mixture to flour nuts and fruit. Add floured raisins, nuts and fruit. Turn into 2 well-greased 9×5″ loaf pans or into well-greased large bundt pan and bake at 325° for 1 hour or until well done. Cool 20 minutes, then turn out on rack. Makes approximately 16 servings.

Mrs. Wm. T. Mehrtens
Destrehan

Dessert Spread

2 — 8 oz. packages cream cheese
½ lb. dates, pitted and chopped
2 tablespoons honey
½ cup cream

Mix all ingredients in food processor or blender.

NOTE: May be served on cookies, crackers or as frosting on cake, etc.

Mrs. A. A. Ardoin, Jr.
Alexandria

Filling and Cake Bake

Cake Bake:

2 sticks butter or oleo
2 cups sugar
3 eggs
3 cups flour
3 teaspoons baking powder
1 cup milk
½ teaspoon salt
½ teaspoon lemon flavoring
½ teaspoon vanilla flavoring
Grated rind of one lemon

Filling:

¼ cup oleo
1 cup coconut
¼ cup lemon juice
¾ cup orange marmalade

Cream butter and sugar. Add eggs to milk, add flavoring and lemon rind. Add baking powder and salt to sifted flour and mix alternately with liquid ingredients into the butter and sugar. Melt ¼ cup oleo, mix coconut, lemon juice and marmalade and put in two 8″ cake pans. Pour batter on top. Bake at 350° for 35-40 minutes. Cool cake 10 minutes, then turn one layer on top of the other, filling side up.

Makes 16 servings.

NOTE: Spread Cool Whip on sides if desired.

Mary Crawford
Coushatta

Cherry Jubilees

2 cups all-purpose flour
1½ cups sugar
2 ozs. (2 sqs.) unsweetened baking chocolate, melted
1 cup margarine or butter, softened
½-1 teaspoon almond extract
4 eggs
21 oz. can prepared cherry fruit filling
3 tablespoons slivered almonds
Powdered sugar

Preheat oven to 350°. Grease bottom of 15×10″ pan. Combine sugar and butter; then add flour, chocolate, eggs and almond extract. Beat 2 minutes at medium speed. Spread in greased pan. Using about 1 tablespoon per serving, spoon cherry filling in 3 rows of five over batter. Sprinkle almonds over filling. Bake at 350° for 25-30 minutes or until top springs back. (Do not overbake.) Cool and dust with powdered sugar.

Makes 15 servings.

Mrs. Paul L. (Kathleen) Erny
Pineville

Italian Fig Cookies

Fig Mixture:
- **5 lbs. dried figs**
- **5 lbs. raisins**
- **2 lbs. nutmeats**
- **1 tablespoon nutmeg**
- **1 tablespoon allspice**
- **1 tablespoon black pepper**
- **6 orange peelings, dried at least one week**
- **1 pint red wine**

Dough:
- **5 lbs. all-purpose flour**
- **1 lb. sugar**
- **4 tablespoons baking powder**
- **1 tablespoon salt**
- **4 eggs, beaten**
- **2¼ cups water, warm**
- **1½ lbs. Crisco or oleo**

Fig Mixture: Cut tips off figs and soak with raisins overnight in pint of red wine. Next day grind all ingredients together and mix well, set aside (overnight).

Dough: Mix together flour, salt and baking powder; work into Crisco. Add sugar which has been dissolved in warm water. Add eggs and salt. Knead the dough well. Roll out in work-size strips, very thin (that's the secret — thin), about 3″ long. Spread with fig mixture, close and roll gently. Cut into desired lengths. Cut niches on sides and small slits on top. Grease cookie sheets. Bake 15 minutes on top shelf and 15 minutes on bottom shelf of oven. Watch very carefully so that cookies will not burn. When they are cool, ice with thin icing and candy topping.

NOTE: The icing can be tinted in different colors, if desired.

Josephine P. Cali
Laplace

Humdingers

1—8 oz. package chopped dates
1 stick oleo
1 cup granulated sugar
1 cup finely chopped pecans
1 teaspoon vanilla
1½ cup rice crispies
1 cup powdered sugar for rolling cookies

Cook first 3 ingredients until just melted and keep warm for a few minutes. Add remaining 3 ingredients, stir and pour onto foil. Spread with spoon so mixture will cook slightly. Shape into balls and roll in powdered sugar. Let stand several hours. These may be stored in airtight containers for several days.

Makes about 3 dozen.

NOTE: These are well-liked by grown-ups and children and may be served at special parties.

Betty Evans
Delhi

Merry Mincemeat Cookies

½ cup shortening
½ cup margarine, softened
½ cup firmly packed brown sugar
¼ cup sugar
1 egg, well beaten
½ teaspoons vanilla
1 — 9 oz. package condensed mincemeat
2½ cups all-purpose flour
1 teaspoon baking powder
½ teaspoon salt

Cream shortening, margarine and sugar until light and fluffy; add egg and vanilla, beating well. Break mincemeat into small pieces and stir into creamed mixture. Combine flour, baking powder and salt; add to creamed mixture, blending well. Chill at least 2 hours. Shape dough into walnut-size balls, and place on lightly greased cookie sheet. Gently press each cookie flat with the bottom of a greased glass. Bake at 400° for 5-8 minutes or until lightly browned. Remove from cookie sheet at once and cool on a rack.

Makes about 6½ dozen.

Mrs. Wendell Murphy
Cameron

Nut Macaroons

2 eggs
½ teaspoon salt
1 teaspoon vanilla extract
1 cup sugar
3 cups pecans, finely ground

Preheat oven to 325°. Put eggs, salt and vanilla extract in large bowl. Beat well for 2 minutes at high speed. Beat in sugar gradually for 1 minute. Add nuts. Blend on low speed. Drop by small teaspoonfuls on well-greased and floured cookie sheet. (Use margarine to grease sheet.) Bake at 325° for 10 minutes.

Mrs. Velma Goudeau
Cottonport

Lemon Snowbars

Crust:
1 cup margarine
½ cup confectioners sugar
2 cups flour

Filling:
4 eggs
2 cups sugar
1 tablespoon flour
½ teaspoon baking powder
⅓ cup lemon juice

Crust: Cream margarine and sugar. Add flour and blend well. Pat into ungreased 13×9×2" pan. Bake at 325° for 15 minutes.

Filling: At once, beat eggs slightly, add sugar, flour and baking powder. Mix well. Add lemon juice; stir, but do not beat. Pour over warm crust. Return to oven. Bake 45 more minutes at 325° or until lightly browned. Sift additional confectioners sugar over top. Let cool completely. Cut into bars or squares.

Jean Briscoe
Luling

Lacy Peanut Crisps

½ cup light corn syrup
½ cup chunk-style peanut butter
⅓ cup butter or margarine
1 cup quick or old fashioned oats, uncooked
½ cup firmly packed brown sugar
¼ cup all-purpose flour
½ cup semi-sweet chocolate, melted

Bring corn syrup to a boil in 2-quart saucepan over medium heat. Add peanut butter and butter; continue cookign over low heat, stirring constantly, until peanut butter and butter are melted and well-blended. Remove from heat; stir in oats, brown sugar and flour. Drop by level teaspoonfuls about 3 inches apart onto greased cookie sheet. Preheat oven to 300° and bake 10-12 minutes. Cool 2 minutes on cookie sheet; gently remove with metal spatula. Cool; drizzle chocolate over cooled cookies.

Makes 3½ dozen.

Connie Abels
Ball

Sesame Seed Cookies

1 stick margarine
2 cups brown sugar
1 egg
1 cup flour
¼ teaspoon salt
½ teaspoon baking powder
1 teaspoon vanilla
⅔-¾ cup sesame seed, toasted

Cream margarine and sugar. Add egg, flour, salt and baking powder, then vanilla. Drop by ½ teaspoon onto greased cookie sheet. Bake at 325° 8-10 minutes. Allow to cool about 1 minute before removing from sheet. Yields about 75 wafers.

NOTE: This is a marvelous wafer-like cookie that is very thin and burns easily, so watch closely.

Mrs. Robert Firnberg
Hodge

Sugar Coolies

1 cup oleomargarine
1 cup sugar
3 eggs
1 teaspoon vanilla
3 cups sifter flour
1 teaspoon soda

Cream oleomargarine, add eggs and vanilla and mix until well combined. Sift dry ingredients together and add cream mixture, mixing thoroughly (if dough is a little too soft, add extra flour). Chill dough for at least 1 hour. Roll out thinly on lightly floured board or between 2 sheets of wax paper. Cut cookies with floured donut cutter and place on baking sheet. Bake at 425° for 6 or 7 minutes.

Antoinette Duhe
LePlace

Grandma's Teacakes

1 cup butter
2 cups sugar
½ teaspoon salt
2 teaspoons baking powder
¼ teaspoon cinnamon
4 cups flour
3 eggs
1 teaspoon vanilla

Cream butter and sugar until light and fluffy. Sift salt, baking powder, cinnamon, and 3 cups of flour together. Add eggs one by one beating well after each addition. Add vanilla. Gradually add the sifted flour mixture. Mix well. Add reserved cup of flour if dough is too soft. Bake at 375° for 12-15 minutes. Roll out dough on lightly floured surface and cut as desired with cookie cutter.

Phyllis L. Dartez
Abbeville

Snickerdoodles

1 cup soft butter
1½ cups sugar
2¾ cups flour
2 teaspoons cream tartar
2 eggs
1 teaspoon soda
¼ teaspoon salt
2 teaspoons cinnamon
2 tablespoons sugar

Cream butter, sugar and eggs. Combine flour, cream tartar, soda and salt and stir into creamed mixture. Blend thoroughly. Form dough into 2″ balls and roll each ball in mixture of cinnamon and sugar. Place on ungreased cookie sheet. Bake 8-10 minutes at 400° Makes 5 dozen.

Suzanne Magee
Slagle

Country Apple Pie

2 cups sifted all-purpose flour
1 teaspoon salt
¾ cup shortening (Crisco)
6 tablespoons water
1 cup sugar
2 tablespoons flour
1 teaspoon cinnamon
Sugar
½ teaspoon ground nutmeg
¼ teaspoon salt
6 cups sliced, pared and cored cooking apples
3 tablespoons butter or margarine
Milk

Sift 2 cups flour and salt into mixing bowl. Cut in shortening with pastry blender until mixture resembles cornmeal. Sprinkle water evenly over mixture. Stir with fork until all flour is moistened. Gather mixture together, shape into a ball. Divide in half. Roll out half the pastry on floured board; cut out a 12-inch circle; fit into a 9-inch pie plate. Combine sugar, 2 tablespoons flour, cinnamon, nutmeg and salt in bowl. Arrange half the apples in pastry lined pie plate. Sprinkle with half the sugar mixture. Repeat with remaining apples and sugar mixture. Dot top with butter or margarine. Roll out remaining pastry; cut 12-inch circle; cut decorative vents to allow steam to escape during the baking. Place over filling; press edges together; form standing rim; flute edge. For a sparkly top, brush top lightly with milk; sprinkle with sugar. Bake at 425° for 40-45 minutes.

Mrs. Robert E. Birdsall
Jonesboro

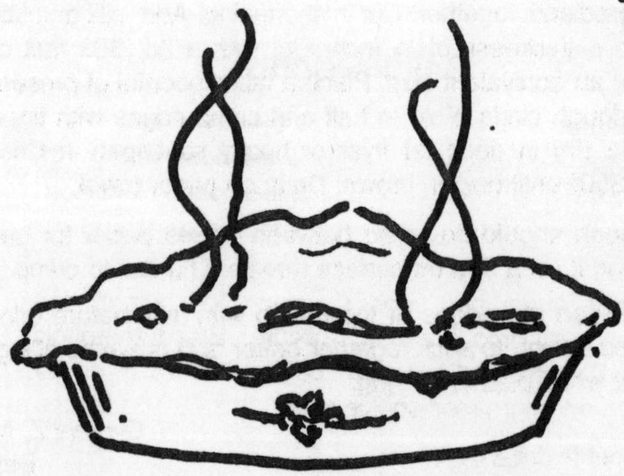

Vanilla Cream Pie

1 cup sugar
3 tablespoons flour
1½ cups milk
3 eggs, separated
¼ cup margarine
1 teaspoon vanilla
1—8″ pie crust, baked

Place sugar and flour in saucepan and mix well. Add milk and mix. Cook over medium heat until very hot, stirring constantly. Place egg yolks in small bowl, beat well with rotary beater. Add a little of the hot milk mixture to eggs and stir; then add this mixture to the first hot milk mixture. Cook over medium-low heat, stirring constantly until thick. Take off fire. Add margarine and vanilla; stir well. Pour into baked pie shell. Beat egg whites with electric mixer until stiff; add ½ cup sugar; continue beating until they are glossy. Pour on top of pie; place in oven to brown at 400° for about 10 minutes.

Makes 6 servings.

Mrs. Elizabeth Allen
Farmerville

Fried Pies

2 cups sifted flour
2 teaspoons baking powder
½ teaspoon salt
6 tablespoons Crisco shortening
⅔ cup milk
½ to ¾ cup preserves
1-1½ quarts Crisco cooking oil

Sift dry ingredients together. Cut in shortening. Add milk and stir well. Roll out to a thickness of ¼ inch. Cut with a no. 303 fruit can or anything of an equivalent size. Place a tablespoonful of preserves in center of dough circle. Fold in half and crimp edges with fingers or with a fork. Fry in deep fat fryer or heavy saucepan in Crisco oil heated to 350° until golden brown. Drain on paper towel.

NOTE: Dough should be rolled between waxed paper for best results. Rolling it on a floured surface makes it harder to crimp.

NOTE: Moisten the edges of the dough with milk before crimping. This causes dough to stick together better and prevents filling from leaking out while pies are frying.

Makes about 2 dozen.

Cynthia Z. Nunez
Bell City

Butter Crunch Lemon Chiffon Crumb Pie

Crust:

½ cup butter
¾ cup dark brown sugar (firmly packed)
1 cup flour
½ cup chopped pecans

Filling:

½ cup sugar
1 tablespoon Knox Gelatin dissolved in ⅔ cup water
4 eggs
⅓ cup lemon juice
1 tablespoon grated lemon rind

Crust: Mix all ingredients with hands. Spread in oblong pan. Bake in hot oven 15 minutes. Stir and break up with fork or spoon into sizable crumbs (save half cup crumbs for topping); press remainder of crumbs against bottom and sides of pie pan. Cool.

Filling: Separate whites from yolks. Beat yolks slightly and combine with other ingredients. Cook over very slow fire stirring constantly until mixture comes to boil and mounds slightly when mixture drops from spoon. Cool. Beat whites until stiff. Add an additional half cup sugar. Fold custard into meringue. Pour on crumbs in pie pan. Refrigerate. Whip half cup heavy cream and put on top of pie. Sprinkle remaining crumbs on top. Refrigerate.

NOTE: A bit of trouble but worth it — *luscious!*

Mrs. J. P. Kelley
Alexandria

Rich Lemon Pie

1 unbaked pie crust
5 egg yolks
1½ cups sugar
¾ cup butter
1 grated lemon rind
5 egg whites
6 teaspoons sugar

Beat egg yolks. Add sugar and blend. Add the soft butter and beat well. Add milk and grated rind. Pour into the unbaked crust and bake at 350° until the filling will not shake. Beat egg whites with 6 teaspoons sugar until very stiff. Spread over pie. Return to oven and brown slightly at 350°.

Mrs. Dorothy Bourn
Winnfield

Mincemeat Chiffon Pie

1 envelope Knox unflavored gelatin
½ cup water
¼ cup rum
3 egg whites
⅓ cup sugar
⅛ teaspoon salt
1 cup heavy cream, whipped
1½ cups prepared mincemeat
9″ baked pastry shell

Sprinkle Knox gelatin over ½ cup water in saucepan. Place over low heat. Stir constantly until dissolved. Remove from heat. Stir in rum and mincemeat. Chill until mixture mounds when dropped from spoon. Beat egg whites until stiff but not dry. Gradually add sugar and salt and beat until very stiff. Fold in gelatin mixture. Fold in whipped cream. Turn into pastry shell. Chill until firm. If desired, garnish with additional whipped cream and sprinkle with nutmeg.

Ann LeJeune
Lafayette

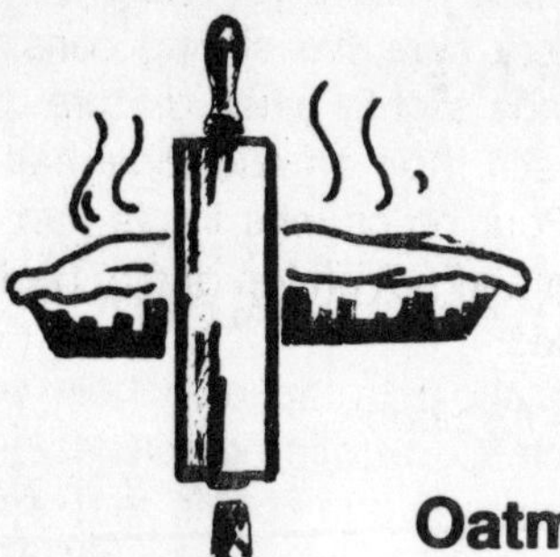

Oatmeal Pie

1 unbaked pie crust
¼ cup oleo
½ teaspoon cloves
½ teaspoon cinnamon
1 cup quick cooking oats
½ cup sugar
1 cup dark Karo syrup
3 eggs
¼ teaspoon salt

Cream oleo and sugar. Add spices and salt. Stir in syrup. Add eggs one at a time and beat well. Stir in oats. Pour into unbaked pie crust. Bake at 350° for 1 hour or until knife comes out clean. Add pecans if desired.

Makes 6-8 servings.

Sandy Fisher
Ruston

Fresh Strawberry Pie

9″ pie shell (baked)
1½ pints fresh strawberries
1 cup sugar
1 cup water
2 tablespoons cornstarch
2 tablespoons white Karo syrup
3 heaping tablespoons strawberry Jello
Whipped topping

Wash and stem strawberries. Allow to drain. Combine sugar, water, cornstarch and Karo syrup in a heavy saucepan. Cook until thick. Remove from heat and add jello. Allow to cool. Pour one-half of mixture into cooled pie shell. Arrange strawberries in pie shell (large berries may be cut in half). Some berries may be reserved to garnish pie. Pour remainder of mixture over berries. Top with whipped topping. Refrigerate until set.

Mrs. George E. (Sonja) Travis
Jackson

Fresh Peach Pie

1 graham cracker pie shell
4 or 5 fresh peaches
1 can apricot nectar
½ cup sugar
3 tablespoons cornstarch
½ pint whipping cream

Peel and slice peaches and fill pie shell. In top of double boiler combine nectar, sugar and cornstarch. Cook, stirring constantly until mixture is thickened. Pour over peaches and cool in refrigerator. Whip cream and spread on top of cooled pie.

Makes 6 servings.

Ann W. Hughes
Jena

Fluffy Peanut Butter Pie

½ cup peanut butter (creamy or crunchy)
8 ozs. cream cheese (softened)
1 cup powdered sugar
½ cup milk
9 ozs. Cool Whip (thawed)
9″ graham cracker crumb crust
¼ cup finely chopped peanuts

Whip cheese until soft and fluffy. Beat in peanut butter and sugar. Slowly add milk blending thoroughly into mixture. Fold Cool Whip into mixture. Pour into prepared crust. Sprinkle with chopped peanuts. Freeze until firm.

Mrs. Marjorie C. Pollard
Leesville

Pecan Pie

1 package (3¼ ozs.) vanilla pudding and pie filling mix
1 can white corn syrup (light Karo)
¾ can evaporated milk
1 egg, slightly beaten
1 can chopped pecans
1 unbaked pie shell

Blend pudding mix and syrup, add milk and egg, mix well. Stir in pecans and pour into unbaked pie crust. Bake at 375° about 40 minutes until top is firm, and *just begins* to crack. Cook 3 hours. Makes 6 servings.

NOTE: This also makes a delicious pie when walnuts or coconut is substituted for pecans.

Joy E. Bradford
Trout

Wonderful Pie

1 cup sugar
¼ cup flour
1 — 16 oz. can red pitted cherries
1 — 8 oz. can crushed pineapple
1 — 3 oz. package cherry Jello
3 sliced bananas
2 Graham cracker crusts
Whipped cream

Cook the sugar, flour, cherries and pineapple until thickened (about 5 minutes). Remove from fire and add the cherry Jello. Cool 15 minutes. Add the 3 sliced bananas and pour into two Graham cracker crusts. Top with whipped cream just before serving.

Makes 14-16 servings.

Mrs. Jonathan Martin
Ringgold

"Talk Time" Doughnuts

2 eggs
1 cup sugar
1 cup milk
5 tablespoons melted shortening
4 cups all-purpose flour
½ teaspoon nutmeg
½ teaspoon salt
½ teaspoon cinnamon
Powdered sugar

Add 1 cup of sugar slowly to 2 beaten eggs. Stir in 1 cup of milk and 5 tablespoons melted shortening. In a separate bowl put 4 cups all-purpose flour (sift before measuring). Resift with ½ teaspoon of cinnamon, ½ teaspoon nutmeg and ½ teaspoon of salt. Mix dry and moist ingredients. Chill the dough slightly and roll to ½" thickness on a lightly floured board. Cut with floured double cutter and fry in deep fat heated to 375° turning each one as it browns. Cool and dust with powdered sugar.

Agnes Kennedy
LaPlace

Apricot Delight

1 box Nabisco sugar wafers, plus ¼ cup melted oleo
¾ cup oleo
1 box powdered sugar
2 eggs
1 teaspoon vanilla
1 cup chopped pecans
1 lb. dried apricots (cooked, cooled and drained)
8 ozs. Cool Whip

Crust: Crush sugar wafers and mix with melted oleo. Put in large oblong pan or two smaller ones. Reserve a few crumbs for topping. Set crust in refrigerator while preparing filling.

Filling: Cream oleo and powdered sugar and add eggs one at a time mixing well. Add vanilla. Cover crumb crust with cream mixture. Sprinkle with chopped pecans. Cover with apricots and Cool Whip. Sprinkle top with a few crumbs. Chill.

Makes 18 servings.

Leaoto Martin
Shreveport

Creole Bread Pudding with Rum Sauce

6 slices bread, cubed
3½ cups milk, divided
4 eggs, separated
½ cup sugar, divided
1 tablespoon vanilla
Pinch salt
¼ cup margarine or butter, melted
½ cup raisins

Combine bread cubes in 1 cup milk; set aside. Beat egg yolks, 6 tablespoons sugar, and remaining 2½ cups milk. Stir in vanilla, salt, butter and raisins. Pour mixture over bread and mix well. Pour into a shallow 2-quart baking dish. Place dish in a pan of hot water. Bake at 300° about 50 minutes or until knife inserted in center comes out clean.

Meringue: Beat egg whites until stiff. Gradually add 2 tablespoons sugar. Spread over pudding. Bake at 350° about 10 minutes till golden.

Rum Sauce: ½ cup sugar, ¼ cup water, 2 tablespoons butter or margarine, 1 tablespoon rum — combine all except rum in saucepan. Boil one minute. Remove from heat; stir in rum. Yields ½ cup. Serve warm.

Makes 6-8 servings.

Mrs. Farmer L. Burns
New Orleans

Flan (Caramel Custard)

3 eggs
⅓ cup sugar
¼ teaspoon salt
2 cups milk, scalded
½ teaspoon vanilla

Beat slightly to mix the first 3 ingredients. Then scald 2 cups of milk. Stir into egg mixture. Add vanilla. Pour into six caramelized heavy pottery custard cups (directions follow recipe). May use a 1-1½ quart baking dish and set in pan of hot water (1″ deep). Bake just until silver knife inserted 1″ from edge comes out clear. (Soft center sets as it stands). Immediately remove from heat. Serve cool or chilled when unmolded melted caramel runs down sides forming a sauce.

To caramelize sugar in custard molds, melt ½ cup sugar in heavy pan over low heat, shaking pan as sugar melts. Heat until melted to a golden brown syrup, stirring constantly. Pour a little melted sugar into each custard cup or baking dish. Move cups or dish about so that caramel will coat sides. When caramel is hard, fill cups or dish with custard recipe.

NOTE: I use low fat milk for this recipe.

Mrs. E. C. Uhrich
Alexandria

Cheese Cake

Crust:
¾ box graham cracker crumbs
1 stick butter
½ cup sugar

Topping:
2 — 8 oz. cartons sour cream
4 tablespoons sugar
2 teaspoons vanilla

Filling:
5 — 8 oz. packages cream cheese
5 eggs, whole
1⅓ cups sugar
Juice of 2 lemons

Melt butter; add crumbs and sugar. Mix well and press up the sides and bottom of spring pan for crust. Beat softened cream cheese in mixer until soft and creamy. Add eggs, one at a time, beating well after each egg. Add sugar and lemon juice. Mix well. Pour into crumb crust. Bake in preheated oven 400° for 20-25 minutes. (Do not brown.) Remove from oven and let cool about 30 minutes.

Topping: Mix sour cream with sugar and vanilla. Blend well and pour over top of cake. Return to oven and bake 10 minutes. Remove and let cool. Place cake in refrigerator at least 3 hours (better overnight).

NOTE: Recipe never fails.

Mrs. Warren S. Anderson
DeRidder

Chilled Marble Cheese Cake

12 Lady fingers, split
1 envelope unflavored gelatin
¼ cup cold water
3 — 8 oz. packages cream cheese (softened)
1 cup sugar
1 — 3¾ oz. package instant chocolate pudding mix
1 — 3¾ oz. package instant vanilla pudding mix
1 teaspoon lemon rind
¼ teaspoon almond extract

Line sides of a 9" spring cake pan with waxed paper; then lady fingers, rounded side out. Set aside. Soften gelatin in cold water. Dissolve over hot water. Place 1½ packages cream cheese in each of two large bowls, beat until smooth. Blend ½ cup sugar and 2 tablespoons dissolved gelatin into each bowl. Set aside. Prepare chocolate and vanilla pudding mixes as directed on packages. Blend the chocolate pudding and almond extract into one cheese mixture. Blend the vanilla and lemon rind into the remaining bowl of cheese mixture. Drop the mixture alternately into the prepared pan to give a marbled effect. Using a knife, lightly score the top to give a pattern. Chill at least 6 hours or until firm. To serve remove sides of pan and wax paper.

Genevieve Kelley
Avoyelles

Crepes Brulatour

8 ozs. cream cheese
¼ cup pecan pieces
½ cup sugar
1 tablespoon vanilla
Frozen strawberries, thawed
Whipped cream

Make 12 crepes from standard recipe. Cream all ingredients together. Place 1 tablespoon mixture on each crepe and roll. Top crepes with strawberries and whipped cream.

Makes 6 servings.

NOTE: Crepes may be flamed with strawberry liqueur or Kirsch.

Hazel C. Gourgues
Hahnville

Cranberry Torte Deluxe

1½ cups graham cracker crumbs
½ cup chopped pecans
¼ cup sugar
6 tablespoons butter or margarine, melted
1½ cups ground fresh cranberries (2 cups whole berries)
1 cup sugar
2 egg whites
1 tablespoon frozen orange juice concentrate, thawed
⅛ teaspoon salt
1 cup whipping cream
3 slices fresh orange (unpeeled and quartered
1 recipe Cranberry Glaze (ingredients listed below)

Cranberry Glaze:

½ cup sugar
1 tablespoon cornstarch
¾ cup fresh cranberries
⅔ cup water

In a mixing bowl combine graham cracker crumbs, pecans, the ¼ cup sugar and the melted butter or margarine; press onto bottom and up sides of an 8″ springform pan. Chill. In large mixer bowl combine cranberries and the 1 cup sugar; let stand 5 minutes. Add unbeaten egg whites, orange juice concentrate, vanilla and salt. Beat on low speed of electric mixer till frothy. Then beat at high speed 6-8 minutes or till peaks form (tips stand straight). In small mixer bowl whip cream to soft peaks (tips curl over); fold into cranberry mixture. Turn into crust. Freeze firm. To serve, remove torte from pan. Place on serving plate. Spoon Cranberry Glaze in center; place orange slices around outside. Makes 8 to 10 servings.

Cranberry Glaze: In saucepan stir together sugar and cornstarch; stir in cranberries and water. Cook and stir till bubbly. Cook, stirring occasionally, just till cranberry skins pop. Cool to room temperature (do not chill). Makes 1 cup.

Leigh Wimberly
Leesville

Whipped Floating Island

4 cups milk
3 eggs, separated
1 cup sugar
¼ cup cornstarch
1 teaspoon vanilla
¼ cup sherry

Scald milk over low heat. In a bowl, combine egg yolks, sugar and cornstarch; beat well. Slowly add hot milk to mixture. Pour mixture into saucepan. Cook, stirring constantly until custard thickens. Remove from heat and let cool. Mix in vanilla and sherry. Very gently, fold in stiffly-beaten egg whites. Chill before serving.

Makes 6-8 servings.

Sandra L. Theall
Abbeville

Chocomint and Berry Dessert

Crust:
⅓ cup melted butter
15 Chocolate Oreo Cookies, crushed

Combine ingredients in a bowl. Press ½ cup of crumb crust on bottom of a foil-lined loaf pan. Freeze. Save remainder of crumb mixture.

Filling:
1 cup Hershey's syrup
1 cup pureed strawberries
4½ cups Cool Whip
2 tablespoons corn syrup
3 — 3 oz. packages softened Philadelphia cream cheese
1 teaspoon peppermint extract

Whip 6 ozs. cream cheese in a mixing bowl. Add chocolate syrup. Blend well. Fold in peppermint extract and 3 cups of Cool Whip. Spoon half this mixture in loaf pan. Top with one half cup crumb mixture. Return to freezer for at least 15 minutes.

In another bowl, add the remaining package of cream cheese. Blend strawberries and corn syrup until smooth. Fold in 1½ cups Cool Whip. Spoon this mixture onto the chocolate layer in loaf pan. Sprinkle with ½ cup crumb mixture. Spoon the rest of the chocolate on. Top with remaining crumbs; press lightly. Cover. Freeze for at least 6 hours. Remove from freezer about 10 minutes before serving. Slice to serve.

Aline Roig
Chalmette

Strawberry Shortcake

3 cups flour
4 teaspoons baking powder
1 teaspoon salt
3 tablespoons sugar
½ cup shortening
1 cup milk

Combine dry ingredients. Fold in shortening. Add milk. Roll out and cut shortcakes. Bake at 400° until lightly brown. Split and fill with strawberries. Cover with whipping cream and serve.

Mrs. R. A. Bennett, Jr.
DeRidder

Pudding Cake

First Layer:

1 cup flour
1 stick oleo
1 cup chopped pecans

Blend all ingredients and press into a 9×13″ greased pan. Bake for 15 minutes at 350°. Cool.

Second Layer:

1 cup powdered sugar
1 — 8 oz. package cream cheese
1 teaspoon vanilla
1 cup Cool Whip

Blend sugar, cream cheese and vanilla; add 1 cup whipped topping and spread over cooled first layer. Chill.

Third Layer:

2 — 3 oz. packages instant chocolate pudding
3 cups cold milk
1 teaspoon vanilla

Beat together these ingredients until smooth. Pour over chilled layers. Top with remainder of the whipped topping. Garnish with grated chocolate if desired.

NOTE: You may substitute pistachio, lemon or coconut pudding, or use both vanilla and chocolate puddings; or add coconut to the topping and use Dream Whip instead of Cool Whip for delightful variations.

Reah Simpson, Farmerville
Mrs. Geneva Griffith, Cameron
Patricia W. Hargrove, Oakdale
Mrs. Elsie Watts, Winnfield
Mrs. Jane Wroten, Winnfield

Delicious Dessert

20-25 graham crackers, crushed fine
½ stick oleo, melted
¼ cup sugar
½ gallon vanilla ice cream
1 cup broken toasted pecans
1 jar Borden's butterscotch sundae sauce

Combine first 3 ingredients and spread in 9×13″ Pyrex dish. Bake 5 minutes at 350°. Cool. Let ice cream stand at room temperature until soft. Fold in toasted pecans and ½ of the butterscotch sundae sauce. Pour into crust. Top with remaining sauce and sprinkle a few pecans on top. Freeze. To serve, remove from freezer and let stand for 15 minutes. Cut in squares.

Mrs. Robert Fenstermaker
Oakdale

Wine Cake Pudding

3 eggs, separated
1¼ cups milk, scalded
½ cup all purpose flour
1 cup sugar
⅛ teaspoon salt
2 tablespoons margarine, melted
¼ cup lemon juice
Grated rind of 1 lemon
¼ cup white wine

Lightly beat egg yolks; add milk, mixing well. Combine flour, sugar and salt in a large mixing bowl; stir lightly. Add egg yolk mixture to dry ingredients along with margarine, lemon juice, lemon rind and wine. Mix well. Beat egg whites until peaks form; fold into egg yolk mixture. Spoon into 6 greased custard cups and place cups in a 13×9×2″ baking pan. Pour 1″ hot water into pan. Bake at 325° for 45 minutes.

Makes 6 servings.

Mrs. Farmer L. Burns
New Orleans

Date Delight

12 Oreo or Hydrax cookies, crushed
1 — 8 oz. package dates, chopped
2 cups small marshmallows
1 cup heavy cream
¾ cup water
¼ teaspoon salt
½ cup chopped pecans
½ teaspoon vanilla

Remove ¼ cup of crumbs. Spread remaining crumbs in 10×6×½″ pan. In saucepan combine dates, water and salt. Bring to a boil. Reduce heat and simmer 3 minutes. Remove from heat and add marshmallows and stir until melted. Cool. Stir in nuts. Spread date mixture over crumbs in dish. Combine cream and vanilla. Whip and spread over mixture. Sprinkle with reserved crumbs. Chill overnight. Cut into squares to serve.

Mrs. J. M. (Valerie) Hester,
Lake Providence

Strawberry Chiffon Squares

⅓ cup butter or margarine
1½ cups finely crushed vanilla
1 — 3 oz. package strawberry gelatin
¾ cup boiling water
1 — 14 oz. can Eagle Brand condensed milk
1 — 10 oz. package frozen sliced strawberries, thawed
4 cups Campfire marshmallows (miniatures)
1 cup (½ pint) whipping cream, whipped

In a small saucepan melt butter. Stir in crumbs. Pat firmly on bottom of 11×7″ baking dish. Chill. In large bowl, dissolve gelatin in boiling water; stir in sweetened condensed milk and undrained strawberries. Fold in marshmallows and whipped cream. Pour into prepared pan. Chill 2 hours or until set. If desired, garnish with topping and strawberries.

Makes 12 servings.

Mrs. Larry Merritt
Sibley

Sweeties Pineapple Custard

3 eggs, separated
5 heaping tablespoons sugar
1 heaping tablespoon + 1 level tablespoon cornstarch
½ teaspoon salt
3 cups diluted evaporated milk
1½-2 teaspoons vanilla extract
1 medium size or 2 small cans crushed pineapple (well-drained)

Beat egg yolks till creamy and light. Add cornstarch and salt. Mix well. Have milk to scalding point. Add ½ of milk to egg mixture, slowly. Pour egg and milk mixture into saucepan with remainder of milk in saucepan. Cook over medium heat, stirring constantly till custard thickens. Do not let mixture boil! Remove from heat; add vanilla. Mix. Add drained pineapple. Pour into 8″ square Pyrex dish.

Top with Meringue:

3 egg whites, stiffly beaten and peaked
3 tablespoons sugar beaten in one at a time.
1 teaspoon vanilla extract.

Place meringue over custard. Bake at 400° for 8 minutes.

Makes 8 servings.

Mrs. Robert D. Jones
Alexandria

Homemade Ice Cream

3 cans condensed milk
1 pint whipping cream
2 pints half and half
1 tablespoon vanilla flavoring

Take 1 pint of milk and heat on top of stove. Add remaining ingredients. Mix well and place in freezer container. You may add any fresh fruit, blended, to this mixture. Makes 1 gallon.

Floye Clegg
Walker

Old-Fashioned Peach Ice Cream

5 eggs
14 oz. can condensed milk
Juice ½ lemon
½ pint heavy whipping cream
3 tablespoons flour
10 or more soft peaches, peeled and mashed
½ gallon milk
1½ cups sugar

Beat eggs in a large bowl. Add lemon juice and ½ gallon milk. In a double boiler, mix flour and sugar. Add the egg-milk mixture and cook until consistency of boiled custard. Let cool and add the condensed milk and whipping cream. Add the peaches. Place in freezer container and add milk to the required level (add more sugar if desired). Then freeze.

Makes 1 gallon

Mrs. Mona Gill Preaus
Farmerville

Perfect Divinity Fudge

2½ cups sugar
2 egg whites
½ cup Karo syrup (white)
½ cup hot water
2 cups chopped pecans

Beat egg whites until stiff. Put sugar in saucepan. Mix ½ cup Karo syrup and ½ cup hot water; stir and mix with sugar. Bring to boil until it forms peaks when dropped in cup of water. Remove from burner and pour into egg whites in mixer. Beat with mixer until hard, then add 2 cups pecans or nuts. Pour in butter greased plate, cut into pieces when cooled well.

Antoinette Duhe
LaPlace

Easter Peanut Butter Eggs

¾ cup peanut butter
1 teaspoon vanilla
1 can sweetened condensed milk
1 teaspoon salt
4 cups powdered sugar

Cream peanut butter, vanilla and salt in medium mixing bowl. Blend in sweetened condensed milk till smooth. Add sugar gradually, blending well after each addition. Blend till mixture is very stiff. Turn onto board, kneed in all remaining sugar carefully. Mixture should be smooth and not sticky. Cut mixture into desired number of pieces. Mold each piece into egg shape with palms of hands. Place each egg on waxed paper-lined cookie sheet. Chill for several hours or overnight. Dip in chocolate dipping recipe.

Chocolate Dipping:

½ pound semisweet chocolate
⅓ to ½ slab household paraffin wax

Place chocolate and wax in top of double boiler. Place over hot water. Cook over medium heat, stirring with wire whisk until chocolate and parafin are melted. *Never melt paraffin over direct heat.* Insert double pronged kitchen fork into bottom of fondant egg or place egg on flat wire skimmer. Dip egg in chocolate. Carefully place each egg on waxed paper-lined cookie sheet. Stir chocolate thoroughly with wire whisk before dipping each egg. If chocolate coating begins to cook and thicken place over low heat. Let chocolate coating dry thoroughly before adding your decorations.

Mrs. Jimmy Presley
Shreveport

Double Divinity Bars

2 cups sugar
⅔ cup water
½ cup light corn syrup
2 egg whites, stiffly beaten
1 teaspoon vanilla
Nuts

Combine ½ cup sugar and ⅓ cup water and cook until mixture forms a soft ball in cold water. Set this mixture aside to cool slightly.In another saucepan, combine corn syrup, remaining water, sugar and cook until mixture forms a hard ball in cold water. After first mixture has cooled slightly, slowly add to egg whites, beating constantly for 1-2 minutes. Add the second syrup mixture in the same way. Stir in vanilla and nuts. Pour into a greased pan and cut into bars when cool.

Mrs. Karen Belanger
Cameron

Chocolate Pralines

1 cup sugar
1 cup brown sugar, firmly packed
½ cup light cream
Dash salt
2 tablespoons butter
2 ozs. unsweetened chocolate (melted)
1 teaspoon vanilla
1 cup pecan halves

Combine sugars, cream and salt. Boil to thread stage (265°), stirring occasionally. Blend in chocolate, butter, vanilla and pecan halves. Cook until soft ball stage (238°). Cool and beat until thickened. Drop by tablespoons onto double thickness of waxed paper.

Mrs. A. E. McKeithen
Hodge

Lagniappe

Here are a few charts and ideas to keep on hand for easy reference. Some will be highly useful and some are for a chuckle.

We hate to say good-bye, so we won't. You have provided us with abundant material for another volume with which we shall return. Again, thanks to all, the cooperation has been extra magnificent.

Remember always — your best tester is your taster!

A HANDY SPICE GUIDE
TO MAKE YOU BECOME A SEASONED SEASONER

ALLSPICE — a pea-sized fruit that grows in Mexico, Jamaica, Central and South America. Its delicate flavor resembles a blend of cloves, cinnamon and nutmeg. USES: (Whole) Pickles, meats, boiled fish, gravies. (Ground) Puddings, relishes, fruit preserves, baking.

BASIL — the dried leaves and stems of an herb grown in the United States and North Mediterranean area. Has an aromatic, leafy flavor. USES: For flavoring tomato dishes and tomato paste, turtle soup; also use in cooked peas, squash, snap beans; sprinkle chopped over lamb chops and poultry.

BAY LEAVES — the dried leaves of an evergreen grown in the eastern Mediterranean countries. Has a sweet, herbaceous floral spice note. USES: For pickling, stews, for spicing sauces and soup. Also use with a variety of meats and fish.

CARAWAY — the seed of a plant grown in the Netherlands. Flavor that combines the tastes of Anise and Dill. USES: For the cordial Kummel, baking breads; often added to sauerkraut, noodles, cheese spreads. Also adds zest to French fried potatoes, liver, canned asparagus.

CURRY POWDER — a ground blend of ginger, turmeric, fenugreek seed, as many as 16 to 20 spices. USES: For all Indian curry recipes such as lamb, chicken, and rice, eggs, vegetables, and curry puffs.

DILL — the small, dark seed of the dill plant grown in India, having a clean, aromatic taste. USES: Dill is a predominant seasoning in pickling recipes; also adds pleasing flavor to sauerkraut, potato salad, cooked macaroni, and green apple pie.

MACE — the dried covering around the nutmeg seed. Its flavor is similar to nutmeg, but with a fragrant, delicate difference. USES: (Whole) For pickling, fish, fish sauce, stewed fruit. (Ground) Delicious in baked goods, pastries and doughnuts, adds unusual flavor to chocolate desserts.

MARJORAM — an herb of the mint family, grown in France and Chile. Has a minty-sweet flavor. USES: In beverages, jellies and to flavor soups, stews, fish, sauces. Also excellent to sprinkle on lamb while roasting.

MSG (MONOSODIUM GLUTAMATE) — is a vegetable protein derivative for raising the effectiveness of natural food flavors. USES: Small amounts, adjusted to individual taste, can be added to steaks, roasts, chops, seafoods, stews, soups, chowder, chop suey and cooked vegetables.

OREGANO — the leaf of a safe bush growing in Italy, Greece and Mexico. USES: An excellent flavoring for any tomato dish, especially Pizza, chili con carne, and Italian specialties.

PAPRIKA — a mild, sweet red pepper growing in Spain, Central Europe and the United States. Slightly aromatic and prized for brilliant red color. USES: A colorful garnish for pale foods, and for seasoning Chicken Paprika, Hungarian Goulash, salad dressings.

POPPY — the seed of a flower grown in Holland. Has a rich fragrance and crunchy, nut-like flavor. USES: Excellent as a topping for breads, rolls and cookies. Also delicious in buttered noodles.

ROSEMARY — an herb (like a curved pine needle) grown in France, Spain, and Portugal, and having a sweet, fresh taste. USES: In lamb dishes, in soups, stews and to sprinkle on beef before roasting.

SAGE — the leaf of a shrub grown in Greece, Yugoslavia and Albania. Flavor is camphoraceous and minty. USES: For meat and poultry stuffing, sausages, meat loaf, hamburgers, stews and salads.

THYME — the leaves and stems of a shrub grown in France and Spain. Has a strong, distinctive flavor. USES: For poultry seasoning, in croquettes, fricassees and fish dishes. Also tasty on fresh sliced tomatoes.

TURMERIC — a root of the ginger family, grown in India, Haiti, Jamaica and Peru, having a mild, ginger-pepper flavor. USES: As a flavoring and coloring in prepared mustard and in combination with mustard as a flavoring for meats, dressings, salads.

TABLE OF EQUIVALENTS

Standard Equivalents:

A few grains ....less than ⅛ teaspoon
1 coffee spoon ....1 teaspoon
60 drops ....1 teaspoon
3 teaspoons ....1 tablespoon
2 tablespoons ....1 fluid ounce
16 fluid ounces ....1 pint
16 ounces ....1 pound
16 tablespoons ....1 cup
1 cup ....½ pint
2 pints ....1 quart
4 cups ....1 quart
4 quarts ....1 gallon
8 quarts ....1 peck
4 pecks ....1 bushel

METRIC CONVERSIONS

COMMON UNITS OF WEIGHT

1 pound ....454 grams
1 kilogram ....1000 grams or 2.2. pounds
100 grams ....3⅓ ounces
1 gram ....1/1000 kilogram or
.001 kilogram or
1000 milligrams
1 milligram ....1/1000 gram or .001 gram or
1000 micrograms

COMMON UNITS OF VOLUME

1 quart, 2 pints or 4 cups ....947 milliters
1 cup, 8 fluid ounces or
16 tablespoons ....237 milliliters
1 fluid ounce ....29.57 milliliters

1 teaspoon	5 milliliters
1 liter	1000 milliliters or 1.06 quarts
100 milliliters	3⅓ fluid ounces
1 milliliter	1 cubic centimeter

COMMON UNITS OF LENGTH

1 inch	2.54 centimeters

COMMON UNITS OF TEMPERATURE

250 degrees fahrenheit	106 degrees centigrade
350 degrees fahrenheit	162 degrees centigrade
450 degrees fahrenheit	218 degrees centigrade

CAKE TROUBLESHOOTING

PROBLEM	POSSIBLE CAUSE
Cake is bready and solid.	Too much flour used.
Cake falls	Insufficient quantity of flour or rising ingredients OR excess temperature OR moving cake in the oven before the cell walls have become firm by the heat after the cake has risen.
Uneven surface	Too much heat used.
Crusting over the top before the mixture has risen to full height	Too much heat used.
Bursting at weakest point	To much heat used.
Coarse-grained cakes	Too much leavening ingredients OR too slow an oven OR insufficient creaming of shortening and sugar OR insufficient beating of batter before adding egg whites.
Heavy cakes	Too slow an oven OR too much sugar or shortening.

TABLE OF EQUIVALENTS

FOOD EQUIVALENTS

Apples	3 pounds	= about 2 quarts, sliced
Baking Powder	1 teaspoon single-acting	= ¾ teaspoon double-acting
Cheese	1 pound	= 4½ cups
Cottage Cheese	1 pound	= 2 cups
Chocolate, unsweetened	1 square (1 oz.)	= 3-4 tablespoons grated chocolate
Cornstarch	1 tablespoon	= 2 tablespoon flour
Crackers, graham	3 cups crumbs	= 30-36 crackers
Crackers, salted	1 cup fine crumbs	= 20 crackers
Dates, pitted	1 pound	= 2 cups
Eggs		
Whole	1 egg	= about 3 tablespoons
	1 cup	= 5-6 eggs
Whites	1 white	= about 2 tablespoons
	1 cup	= 8-10 whites
Yolks	1 yolk	= about 1 tablespoon
	1 cup	= 14-16 yolks
Figs, chopped	1 pound	= 3 cups
Flour, unsifted	1 pound	= 3 cups
All-purpose, sifted once	1 pound	= 3¾ cups
Cake, sifted once	1 pound	= 2 cups
Gelatin, unflavored	1 envelope (Knox)	= 1 tablespoon
Lemon	1 average size	= 2-3 tablespoons juice, 3 tablespoons rind
Lentils	1 cup dry	= 2 cups cooked
Macaroni	1-1¼ cups dry (4 oz.)	= 2¼ cups cooked
Marshmallows	½ pound	= 30 standard size
	1 standard size	= 10 miniature
Noodles	1½-2 cups dry (4 oz.)	= 2¼ cups cooked
Prunes, dried	1 pound, dried	= 2½ cups
	1 pound, cooked	= 4 cups
Punch	1 gallon	= serves approx. 20
	12 quarts	= 96 punch glasses
Raisins	1 pound seeded	= 2½ cups
	1 pound seedless	= 3 cups
Rice	1 cup raw	= 3-3½ cups cooked
	1 cup pre-cooked	= 2 cups
Shortening, Butter	1 pound	= 2 cups
	½ pound	= 2 sticks
	1 stick	= ½ cup or 8 tablespoons
Spaghetti	1-1¼ cups raw (4 oz.)	= 2½ cups cooked
Sugar		
Brown, sieved and packed	1 pound	= 2⅛ cups
Confectioners' sifted	1 pound	= about 4 cups
Granulated	1 pound	= 2⅛ cups
Yeast	1 cake yeast	= 1 level tablespoon active dry
	1 package dry yeast	= 1 level tablespoon active dry
Vanilla Wafers	1 cup crumbs	= about 22 wafers
Zweibach	1 cup crumbs	= 8-9 slices

HAPLESS HINTS FOR HOPELESS HOUSEWIVES

Thaw fish in milk. The milk draws out the frozen taste and provides a fresh caught flavor.

* * * * * *

To get rid of the "canned taste" in canned shrimp, soak them in a little sherry and 2 tablespoons of vinegar about 15 minutes.

* * * * * *

If your soup or stew is too salty, add cut raw potatoes and discard once they have cooked and absorbed the salt. If too sweet, add salt or a teaspoon of cider vinegar.

* * * * * *

Gravy hints — A different way of browning flour is to put some flour into a custard cup and place beside meat in oven. Once the meat is done the flour will be nice and brown, ready to make a rich, brown gravy.

* * * * * *

When boiling potatoes, add milk to water — about ½ cup to 2 quarts of water — improves flavor, keeps potatoes white.

* * * * * *

No "fry pan explosions" if you sprinkle a little salt in the pan first before starting to fry food.

* * * * * *

Cauliflower keeps white if you put a tablespoon of lemon juice or white vinegar in the cooking water.

* * * * * *

Soggy mashed potatoes — Overcooked potatoes can become soggy when the milk is added. Sprinkle with dry powdered milk for the fluffiest mashed potatoes ever.

* * * * * *

Soften brown sugar by placing a slice of soft bread in the package and closing tightly, in a couple of hours the brown sugar will be soft again.

* * * * * *

Before measuring honey or other syrups, oil the cup with cooking oil and rinse in hot water.

* * * * * *

Hard-boiled eggs are easier to peel if quickly dipped in cold water after boiling. Then let them drain on paper toweling before peeling.

* * * * * *

Don't crowd your oven. Place pans no less than one inch from the oven walls. Heat must circulate freely for best results.

HOW TO WHITEN CLOTHES:

Pour one gallon HOT water into a plastic container(enamel or stainless containers are acceptable, *but do not, repeat,* **DO NOT** use an aluminum pan.

Add one cup of automatic dishwashing compound and one-fourth cup of bleach. STIR WELL.

Into this put your 100 per cent white cotton garments and let them soak for 30 minutes. Wash as usual. Add some white vinegar to the rinse water and the garments will come out snowy white.

If you use this formula for white uniforms or other apparel containing nylon, DO NOT soak in hot water as it sets wrinkles. Mix as above using hot water but let it cool before adding the laundry.

Do not stir the mixture while the clothes are soaking, and do not reuse the same mixture once it has become discolored. Pour it out and start a-fresh.

NEWSPAPER LOGS TO USE IN FIREPLACE:

Fold newspapers in half and make a stack about one inch high, alternating the folded side and the leaf side.

Roll them as tightly as possible, making a log approximately five to six inches in diameter.

Tie them at each end with wire. Don't use cord or string as the cord might burn through, allowing burning paper to either go up the chimney or be blown into the room. These logs are ready to use as is but if you soak them in water and let them dry thoroughly before using, they will burn longer.

GRANDMA'S RECIPE FOR DOING FAMILY WASH:

This is an authentic "washday recipe" in its original spelling as it was written out for a bride four generations ago.

1. Bild a fire in back yard to heet the kettle of rain water.
2. Set tub so smoke won't blow in eyes if wind is pert.
3. Shave one hole cake lie soap in biling water.
4. Sort things, make three piles, 1 white pile, 1 pile cullords, 1 pile work britches and rags.
5. Stir flour in cold water to smooth, then thin down with biling water.
6. Rub dirty spots on board, scrub hard, then bile. Just rench and starch.
7. Take whit things out of kettle with broom stick handle, then rench, blew and starch.
8. Spred tee towels on grass.
9. Hang old rags on fence.
10. Pore rench water on flower beds.
11. Scrub porch with hot soapy water.
12. Turn tubs upside down.
13. Go put on clean dress—smooth hair with side combs, brew cup of tee—set and rest and rock a spell and *count blessings.*

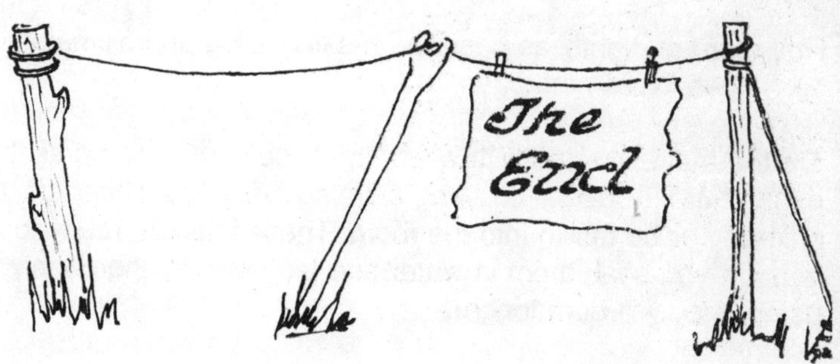

Index

OTHER DESSERTS

PARTY FOODS

VEGETABLES

ORDER FORM

Published by
CLAITOR'S PUBLISHING DIVISION
3165 S. Acadian at I-10, P.O. Box 3333
Baton Rouge, La. 70821

Date ______

Please send __ copy(ies) American Cancer Society A LOUISIANA SAMPLER @ $6.50*

Also send:

__ copy(ies) Vidrine QUELQUE CHOSE de DOUX (Acadian Recipes for the Sweet Tooth) @ $2.00.*

__ copy(ies) La. Federation of Women's Clubs A TASTE OF LOUISIANA @ $7.95.*

__ copy(ies) Jones RECIPES FROM MISS LOUISE @ $7.95.*

__ copy(ies) Jones GORMET'S GUIDE TO NEW ORLEANS Creole Cookbook and Restaurant Guide @ $3.95.*

__ copy(ies) COOK WITH MARIE LOUISE @ $4.95.*

__ copy(ies) Bardwell MODERN MEATLESS MENUS COOKBOOK @ $1.50.*

__ copy(ies) Vidrine LOUISIANA LAGNIAPPE @ $7.95 *

__ copy(ies) Vidrine BEAUCOUP BON @ $3.95.*

__ copy(ies) Vidrine QUELQUE CHOSE PIQUANTE (Spicy Acadian recipes) @ $2.50.*

__ copy(ies) Vidrine QUELQUE CHOSE POUR UN JOYEUX NOEL (Acadian recipes for Christmas) @ $2.00.*

__ copy(ies) Uhler CAJUN COUNTRY COOKIN' @ $3.95.*

__ copy(ies) Uhler ROYAL RECIPES FROM THE CAJUN COUNTRY @ $3.95.*

__ copy(ies) Land LOUISIANA COOKERY @ $3.50.*

__ copy(ies) Guidry From Mamma To Me: ACADIAN-CAJUN RECIPES OF CHURCH POINT, LA. @ $3.95.*

__ copy(ies) Riehl, Mary Alice F., et al. CAJUN ACCENT: A Collection of Recipes in the Acadian Tradition. 1979. @ $4.95.*

__ copy(ies) BRUSHY BAYOU RECIPES @ $9.95.*

__ copy(ies) Ramsey JUST A MOUTHFUL COOKBOOK. 1978. @ $3.95.*

Claitor's BOOKS

☐ Check enclosed, including tax plus 75¢/book del. & ins.

☐ Charge my established account

☐ Send COD

☐ Charge my BankAmericard/VISA

Name ______

Address ______

City ______ State ______ Zip ______

Acct. No. ______ (expires ______)

or Master Charge

Acct. No.. ______ (expires ______)

Interbank No. (M.C. only) ______

*Add tax as appropriate